Markers of Successful Global Leaders:
What Accounts for Their Capacity to Navigate the Complexity of Their Roles?

by

Louise A. Korver

I0415477

Abstract

Global organizations are urgently seeking ways to identify and develop a pool of leaders ready to lead their global operations. This global economic imperative inspired this study's contribution to strategic talent management. The journey through which cognitive and emotional skills develop kindles successful global leaders. This study presents a roadmap of the journey by reporting the antecedents of global leadership ability. When used for selection, these antecedents may contribute to closing the talent gap. The reported experiences are particularly helpful in developing the skills to navigate the complicated process of leading people, processes, and systems in complex, multinational organizations. The study reports *markers* of successful global leaders, which may help organizations refine selection criteria for those with the capacity for global senior executive leadership roles. These *markers* include leadership characteristics and life experiences and report a deontological framework developed through 10 vital experiences and 9 competencies developed through life and work challenges. These markers emerged through a mixed-method focused on narrative analysis from life story interviews coupled with quantitative analysis of validated psychometrics. The study concludes that transformative learning and identity are one and the same: that certain transformational life experiences were structural, changing the perspective and identity of the individuals while evolving the leaders' capacity for global leadership, as reported by recognized measures of self-actualization, global leadership success, and global leadership competency. This study is situated in transformative learning (TL) theory with an emphasis on the transformative life experiences that affect identity, the identity literature within personality psychology, and the specialized field of global leadership within the management and leadership literatures.

KEY WORDS: transformative learning theory, identity development, global leadership, senior management, life story, narrative, strategic talent management

Acknowledgements

This study is the culmination of a life-long goal which would not have been possible without the sustained support of many members of the Fielding community. I would first like to express my appreciation to my supervisory team: Chair of my Committee, Dr. Lenneal Henderson, for his dedicated support of this year-long effort; Mentor and First Reader, Dr. Barbara Mink, who mentored me throughout my Fielding journey; Faculty Reader Dr. Jean-Pierre Isbouts, an inspired writer and thoughtful scholar who provided stimulating feedback that challenged my thinking, and my Student Reader Shelli Hendricks, my trusted colleague and friend. I am humbled by the opportunity to engage with this distinguished group of scholars.

I would also like to acknowledge and thank my External Examiner, Dr. Michael Tucker, whose deep appreciation of global leadership led to the validation of two important instruments used in this study: the GLTAP and GBE. Our discussions about his research and current thinking were seminal for me. A special appreciation also goes to Dr. William Sparks, the creator of the Actualized Leadership Profile who created the validated instrument used to quantify the self-actualization, shadow personality, and motive factors of the study participants.

In addition, I would like to recognize Dr. John Bennett, Associate Professor, Business and Behavioral Science, Wayland H. Cato, Jr. Chair of Leadership, Director, Graduate Programs at the McColl School of Business. He has been an incredibly supportive scholar, mentor, and coach for many years throughout my Fielding journey. High recognition also goes to Anita Hains in her capacity as my research assistant. She supported multiple coding cycles to improve the outcomes of this study.

A big thanks to the transcription team from DCA, Inc., who ensured excellent transcription of the extensive recordings of global leaders with many foreign accents and unique business terms, city names, and descriptions of intensely private, transformative experiences in their stories that brought many typists to tears during the transcription. I am eternally indebted to all those who helped make this dream a reality.

Finally, a prayer of gratitude to my late Mother Grace who unquestionably taught me the persistence and sheer grit to complete this important work. Wherever Gracie is in heaven: *Mom, we have a doctor in the family!*

Dedication

This study is dedicated to my late husband, Douglas Swanson, who left the world's stage in January of 2010 with an unfinished agenda. Yet, in death, Doug has inspired me to try to understand how individuals search for meaningfulness, although he lost his struggle for his own. This poem about perspective transformation has inspired this study.

I am standing upon the seashore. A ship at my side spreads his white sails to the morning breeze and starts for the blue ocean. He is an object of beauty and strength and I stand and watch him until at length he hangs like a speck of white cloud just where the sea and sky come down to mingle with each other. Then someone at my side says, "There! He's gone."

Gone where? Gone from my sight – that is all. He is just as large in mast and hull and spar as he was when he left my side, and just as able to bear his load of living freight to the place of destination. His diminished size is in me, not in him and just at the moment when someone at my side says, "There! He's gone," there come other voices watching him coming, and other voices ready to take up the glad shout, "There! He comes! (Anonomous, n.d.)

Table of Contents

Chapter One: Introduction..1

Chapter Two: Literature Review.........................6

Transformative Learning Theory 8

    Cognitive Developmental Theories/Psycho-
Developmental Approach...............................12

    Criticisms of Transformative Learning Theory..........18

The Link Between Transformative
Learning and Identity......................................23

How Identity Theory Evolved with TL 27

Leadership Theory 31

    Definition of the Global Leader...........................32

    Tasks of Global Leaders...............................32

    The Study of Global Leaders in Their Organizational
Setting 41

    The Link Between Global Leadership and Identity ..42

    Leadership in the Context of Commercial
Requirements...45

Summary and Working Conceptual
Framework for the Study 47

Chapter Three: Research Methodology 51

Introduction to the Inquiry Method....................51

Participant Selection Design 53

    How Research Participants Were Recruited..........53

    Sources of Participants for This Study 54

    Ensuring That Participants Are Exemplars.............58

Recruiting Results 58

Process to Collect Interview Data 58

Data Collection Procedures...60

    The Life Story Interview 60

Narrative Interview Coding Procedures 61

    Interview Coding Results 62

Narrative Interview Analysis 64

Summary of Research Methodology.............................66

Chapter Four: Report of Data and Study Findings...........67

Selection Results...67

    The Caligiuri Selection Report 67

    GLTAP Selection Results 68

    GBE Selection Results..68

    Summary of the Selection Process........................69

Special Considerations for Selection.............................70

Demographics of the Selected Participant Group...........71

Interview Findings 74

Other Findings..78

Reported Findings from the Psychometric
Assessments 88

    Global Business Experience (GBE) Analysis...........88

    Global Leader Tucker Assessment
    Profile (GLTAP) Analysis 93

    Results of the Actualized Leader Profile (ALP) 100

Chapter Five: Significance of the Findings......................110

The Markers of Successful Global Leaders 118

Promising Future Research...122

    Predictive Model of Potential Capacity to Lead
    Globally 122

    Self-Actualization and Social Desirability:
    A Paradox That Needs More Study........................122

The Age-Related Motivators
of the Senior Global Leader 124

The "Uber" Global Leader 125

Questioning the Importance of Language Skills.....125

Successful Outcomes of Business Experience......127

The Significance of the Findings 128

Significance of the Findings for the Literature........128

Significance of the Findings
for the Central Research Question.........................130

Significance of the Findings for Leadership
Development Practice...131

Significance of the Key Concepts 133

Key Methodological Insights of the Study..............134

Significance of the Findings as the Newly
Minted Scholar/Practitioner/Global Leader 135

List of Appendices

Appendix A   Recruiting Brief for Potential Participants 144

Appendix B   Participant Selection Letter 147

Appendix C   Codebook 148

Appendix D   Script to Exclude Potential Participants................151

Appendix E   Informed Consent Form......................................152

Appendix F   Caligiuri's 10 Tasks of Global Leaders
             as a Participant Selection Tool 156

Appendix G   The GLTAP Social Desirability Scale Items...........157

Appendix H   The McAdams Life Story Interview Categories 158

List of Tables

Table 1   Mezirow's 10 Phases of Transformative
Learning 13

Table 2   A Comparative View of the 20th Century
Manager with the 21st Century Global Leader........36

Table 3   The GLTAP Assessment Framework......................41

Table 4   Online Demographic Survey collected through
Survey Monkey...73

Table 5   GLTAP Demographics...73

Table 6   Meta Themes from the Coded Experiences...........75

Table 7   Top Five Categories of Coded Life
Experiences by Weighting of 1,472 Events............76

Table 8   Matrix of Transformative and
Identity-Changing Experiences 79

Table 9   Tracing Experiences that Motivated
TL and Identity Change 83

Table 10   Descriptive Statistics for the GLTAP
(4 variables)...99

Table 11   Descriptive Statistics for the GLTAP
(6 variables)...99

Table 12   Self-Actualization (ALP) Comparison
to GLTAP and GBE...101

Table 13   Age Correlation to ALP Self-Actualization
and Motive Behaviors...103

Table 14   The "Shadow" of the "Achiever"–
Motivated Leader Style.......................................108

Table 15 Korver Model of Potential Capacity
to Lead Globally (Markers).....................................119

Table 16 Pearson r GLTAP Competencies
and ALP Self-Actualization....................................124

Table 17 Full Sample Correlations for the
Caligiuri Global Leader Tasks..............................127

Table 18 Correlation of the GBE and Caligiuri
10 Tasks of Global Leaders...................................128

Table 19 Correlation of Caligiuri Scale and
GBE (Pearson r)..129

List of Figures

Figure 1.   A depiction of Petrieglieri & Stein's
Leader Identity Assessment. 45

Figure 2.   Participant selection criteria and process. 55

Figure 3.   Caligiuri Scale mean values of participants..........70

Figure 4.   Levels of severity of transformative
events across the lifespan. 78

Figure 5.   Identity transformation by reported age...............80

Figure 6.   Transformations reported by participants. 81

Figure 7.   Tracing experiences that motivate
TL and identity change (John). 84

Figure 8.   Profile for success in global leadership as
measured by GBE. 89

Figure 9.   GBE: Driving Performance Results
for this cohort..90

Figure 10. GBE: Building Team Effectiveness
results for this cohort. 91

Figure 11. GBE: Global Networking results
for this cohort..92

Figure 12. Highest reported score for competencies............94

Figure 13. Lowest reported score for competencies.............95

Figure 14. Scattergram of the GLTAP competencies............96

Figure 15. Over/Under GLTAP 1 SD...................................97

Figure 16. Net effective difference scores
from the GLTAP norms. 98

Figure 17. Social desirability compared to
self-actualization measure. 100

CHAPTER ONE

Introduction

Global competitiveness is an economic imperative for international, multinational, transnational, supranational, and global organizations. Despite the challenges of managing across cultures, geographies, and legal entities to achieve competitive advantages, global leaders are required to find solutions in ambiguous and volatile operating conditions when there are few clear answers and many options appear to have high levels of risk. Very few organizations are satisfied with their leaders' abilities to manage across cultures and geographies (Tucker, Bonial, Vanhove, & Kedharnath, 2014). The talent pool for the type of leader who is successful in these complex and often paradoxical operating environments is small, and organizations are urgently seeking ways to identify and develop a pool of leaders ready to handle global expansion plans.

The purpose of this study is to examine whether life experiences may hold significant value in accelerating the development of global leadership ability in general, and particularly the special skills and behaviors of global leaders. The study critically examines transformative learning experiences across the lifespan with specific attention to the effects those experiences have had on identity development. This project studies how identity develops over a lifetime and what role specific transformative experiences may have had in accelerating the development of cognitive and emotional skills.

This project is designed to examine the journey through which cognitive and emotional skills develop, which might help identify the *antecedents* of leadership ability. The study is particularly interested in identifying when and how the ability to navigate the complicated process of global decision making involving people, cultures, and systems within an organization may have been developed. The literature suggests that the experiences which trigger transformation may also affect identity, and the types of events that provoke transformation may provide clues to the characteristic *markers* of identity changes that prepare an individual for increasingly complex experiences and roles.

Global leadership skills apparently develop along a learning path that includes specialized knowledge, skills, and abilities, including a highly developed tolerance for "managing complexity" (Osland, Osland, Bird, & Oddou, 2007). To move forward in today's ambitious, competitive climate, which is operating in volatile, uncertain, complex, and ambiguous (VUCA) conditions – real or perceived – leaders need to continue to challenge their thinking. Harvard cognitive psychologist Dr. Robert Kegan has provided a thread of research in cognitive reasoning and emotional capacity. Most of Kegan's models are stage theories, suggesting that there are levels of intercultural competencies (worldview, social interpersonal style, and situational approach) and cognitive abilities (personality and motives) that develop over time (Kegan, 1994). Kegan's theories are the foundation for many studies about how an individual might gain perspective from complex lived experiences (Pinkavova, 2010). The current study uses these stage theories to claim that by examining the journey through which cognitive and emotional skills develop might help identify the *antecedents* of global leadership ability.

What might we learn about early life experiences that seem to predispose leaders for global leadership success? What if there were early childhood/adolescent *markers* that predisposed individuals to adult global leadership success? If we applied these *markers* to a prospective early career talent pool, how might this suggest a series of assignments and experiences, or a "life curriculum," to accelerate development faster or earlier? This study identified such a set of markers that may help to identify global talent pools, and this is beneficial for emerging leaders, academic curricula for adolescent, high school, and college students, as well as corporate universities and talent management practices in organizations.

The outcome of this research is the identification of when and how successful senior leaders developed the capacity, capability, and competence to lead their global organizations. Early transformative learning episodes support development of the skills needed to successfully lead across many geographies, cultures, languages, and differences. The nature of transformative learning experiences and critical leadership skills required for successful global leaders are identified. The central value of this study is identifying the specific markers of successful global leaders that account for their capacity to navigate the complexity of their roles.

This study embraces the definition by Illeris (2014) that transformative learning is a key form of identity development. To learn more about these phenomena, this study explores the life history of 15 mid-life adults to both locate the antecedents of consciousness transformations (Mezirow, 1978; Kegan, 1994) and describe the links between those experiences to their identity development as they describe and explain them (Illeris,

2014). The participants are organizational leaders, selected based on the depth and breadth of their social, cultural, and individual ability to successfully carry out global responsibilities as senior executives in general management roles within a variety of multinational organizations.

Utilizing narrative inquiry and thematic analysis, the study uses the insights and reflections of participants to advance a working theory of the connections between identity development and transformative learning in developing leaders for complex global roles. The study contributes to the transformative learning literature by describing how particular life events are connected to identity formation in leaders. It reports a set of experiences that contribute to development at different life and career stages. The study classifies the characteristics of experiences, emotions, and mindsets that predispose individuals to a career as a global leader. In taking the life history of successful global executives, this study contributes to the global leadership literature by investigating the role identity development plays across an executive's lifespan and career. One aim is to incorporate this theory into practical leadership development strategies to reduce the shortage of qualified leaders for these complex global leadership roles. This theory may be applied to establish selection criteria for the most promising emerging leaders at any level who can enter the talent pipeline for senior global operating roles.

In order to address the critics of transformative learning (Daloz, 2000; Newman, 2012) who question the likelihood that a single dramatic disorienting dilemma is the cause of a perspective transformation, this study employed a life history interview as the central data collection methodology. This allowed the researcher to look deeply at particular periods in a person's life to grasp the perspective shift as it occurred in various contexts (e.g., to trace the roots of the identity, consciousness, and change in meaning making through the context of one's life both before, during, and after the claimed shift in perspective). This study leaves open the possibility that these shifts may be contributory rather than causal or determinative. Relying substantially on the accounts of participants to determine how causal these shifts were, the study examines the cumulative effects of transformative experiences on identity formation across the life cycle of leaders and answers the research question: ***What are the markers of successful global leaders that would account for their capacity to navigate the complexity of their roles?***

The intent of the study is to: (a) Organize a critical review of the literatures related to this question, (b) design a study that creates a way to collect stories and key observations of global leaders who have undergone a lifetime of transformative learning and identity change, and (c) show the findings and conclusions that will answer the research question.

CHAPTER TWO

---×<·◦◉◦·>×---

Literature Review

Given that the purpose, intention, and context of this chapter is to critically examine and conceptualize the learnings from the literatures, this chapter is organized into three distinct sections, giving equal focus to the three literatures. Throughout the chapter, attention will be paid to identifying the possible theoretical linkages between the three literatures. The chapter then concludes with how the three major concepts are interrelated. This study is situated in transformative learning (TL) theory from 1994 through 2017, with an emphasis on the transformative life experiences that affect identity, the identity literature within personality psychology from 1995 through 2017, and the specialized field of global leadership within the international business management and leadership literatures from 2007 to 2017.

This study proposes that examining the journey through which cognitive and emotional skills develop across the lifespan might help to identify the *antecedents* of leadership ability. A consideration for the framework of this study is a leader's identity—that is, that the leader's identity represents an integration not only of who that person is but also what he or she does in the world, and how those two things are made more congruent. As a result, it is necessary to place the study in its context (e.g., lifespan analysis) to see the antecedents, critical reflections, and conscious actions that appear as the visible manifestations (outcomes) of TL. The use of life story interviewing contributes a holistic view of the individual's developmental opportunities across the lifespan.

Situations that challenge unconscious and embedded points of view through adult interpersonal experiences may create cognitive dilemmas through which the individual develops a relationship with his/her unconscious self (Kegan, 1994; Mezirow, 1998). Through social feedback loops, it is possible for individuals to make their unconscious habits of mind conscious (Mezirow, 1998), if they possess an openness to feedback and reflection. This iterative *feedback/questioning self/decision to change* process may expose the individual to awareness of points of view that no longer contribute to their favorable interactions with others or serve their life purpose (Mezirow, 1998). This process holds the possibility of provoking change in the construction of meaning perspectives, may test unconscious habits of mind rendering them conscious, and may afford a choice point for conscious, emotional change (Kegan, 1994).

To examine these claims, the literature proceeds from a foundational review of TL theories, most notably from Kegan (1994) and Mezirow (1998) to Dirkx (2012) and Illeris (2014) to build the argument that transformative learning allows one to rework one's identity through significant experiences in life. The identity literature provides additional insight into the process of identity development. It is useful to this study to understand the theoretical bridging that occurs between developmental psychologists in TL and personality psychologists about TL and identity development. This theory bridging brings together Jung, Maslow, and McClelland to join the personality and the personality shadow (Jung), self-actualization (Maslow), and motivational drivers (McClelland) that relate to the phenomenon of identity development. Finally, the links between identity and the leadership context are examined in the global leadership literature, positing a standpoint from which to answer the research question: *What are the markers of successful global leaders that would account for their capacity to navigate the complexity of their roles?*

Transformative Learning Theory

Transformative learning (TL), as a theory, was introduced by Paulo Freire during a time of significant social change. His contributions to understanding the emancipatory power of education for ordinary people in societies ripe with dissent were revolutionary (Morrow, 2002, p. 45). His research produced the concept of conscientization. Of critical importance to Freire was "distantiation," using subject-object unity in subject-subject relations (communication) versus technical control through a highly rational, scientifically based ideology that produced a power-based education (p. 54). This breakthrough theory held the most significant benefits for adult learners, as it led to the movement we now call *adult learning theory*. Thus, learning has become a means of transforming adult lives—economically and socially.

Mezirow's theory of TL is perhaps the best known but also, in his own words, "generate[d] so many divergent interpretations" (Mezirow, 1994, p. 221). Mezirow (1978) was interested in the phenomenon of how adult learning motivated individuals beyond the acquisition of sheer knowledge and skill. Mezirow's sense was that knowledge and skills are inherent in the learning process. His term, *instrumental* learning, described the knowledge and skill portion of the learning process. Mezirow's definition of TL, by contrast, created a new sense of freedom or emancipation from old ways of thinking about education which opened an entirely new frame of reference. Mezirow conceptualized this learning process "as a continuum for learning that moves from the acquisition of new knowledge and skill, to elaborating on the existing knowledge, to revising meaning schemes, and to transforming habits of mind. The continuum represents a difference in degree" (Cranton & Kasl, 2012, p. 394). Mezirow prescribed 10 steps of TL, and using these criteria differentiated this learning from *instrumental* learning. TL-type learning affected not only the individual's thinking, but also his/her life experiences, often leaving the individual hungry for more individual learning and growth. TL is both an epistemologically as well as ontologically different space than instrumental learning yet, until Mezirow, there was no method to study it nor a set of practices to develop it in adult learners until 1978.

When Mezirow described the "perspective transformation" he focused on how the learner became disturbed by something that didn't make sense—it is like the sand in the oyster of life— and the psyche became aroused and motivated, which promoted the opportunity for TL. There is both a psychological dimension of perspective transformation and a psychodynamically oriented issue—it is disturbing to a person's profound sense of self. At that point of arousal, the person feels unable to fit the new situation into a known framework or perspective that previously fit. The reservoir of easy, logical answers that previously fit this type of situation no longer does. This is disturbing. The "trigger" event or situation is all about the perturbation that launches the transformation. It is near to impossible to ignore the new perspective one has developed in these situations. Dirkx (2012) stated that the "more fully integrated the presence of this inner world [is] with what we experience from without . . . we are inevitably drawn to the spiritual implications of our learning, life, and work" (p. 128). So, the capacity for TL and perspective transformation is always there, latently, in every aspect of our lives. All that is needed for TL to occur is an openness to taking the risk of change, of making the unconscious conscious. A learning environment may support a sense of safety that encourages, allows, or supports risk-taking.

"The dynamics involved in these TL processes are reflected in Mezirow's 1991 elaboration of psychic distortions and how, through critical reflection, we may become more aware of their presence and influence in our lives" (Dirkx, 2012, p. 403). Piaget's regulation of perceptual distortions is somehow connected in the cycle of making the unconscious conscious and could develop the intellect. Whether this is true or not, individuals who can interpret situations more quickly are often seen as smarter (e.g., more intelligent).

Developmental learning theories have one element that this study will not wholly address: "[P]erceptual development as part of mental growth in general" (Piaget, 1950, p. 88). Through Piaget's many experiments "a close affinity between perception and intellectual activity" (p. 89) appears, and that "perceptual activity . . . constitutes a regulation of perceptional distortions" (p. 89) that "increases with age" (p. 94). Over time, our perceptions become part of our motor skills (in this case, automatic responses to stimulus between people) and therefore habits of mind (Piaget, 1950). This study did not address the development of this intellectual activity, or intelligence per se, and instead sought the task of separating conscious actions from unconscious responses that represented learned behavior, despite those actions being provoked by perceptions. This approach establishes a method of regulating "perceptual distortions" (Piaget, 1950, p. 89), Piaget might say. For this study, the most critical developmental learning theories pertain to transformation and change in a person's perceptions.

TL is about "a social context but. . . [i]t is just that it is not *just* [sic] about the social and material world, but about our *experience* [sic] of it and its influence on our consciousness and our identity that creates the TL. Society raises our consciousness. Consciousness raises our learning opportunities" (Dirkx, 2012, p. 402). Cognitive awareness is required for self-reflection to occur, as is the motivation to examine that newfound awareness.

Despite the theoretical assertions that TL progresses through steps (Mezirow) or stages (Kegan), Erickson (2007) claims that "little work has been done to explore *how* learners know the process of transformational learning by specifically examining their underlying system of meaning construction" (p. 77). This study describes in what ways the phenomenon of transformative learning occurs by examining meaning construction and how it changes throughout life. This provides not only descriptive elements of the transformative experiences and actions but the private reflective processes that underly them. The study also examines different time frames in the life journey to see whether there is any capacity building being developed for transforming, as well as what the TL process looks like at different life stages.

Cognitive Developmental Theories/Psycho-Developmental Approach

The theoretical hypotheses of Mezirow and Kegan, both of whom present arguments within the context of cognitive, rational theory, suggest that experience (no matter how provoked) has the power to transform our belief structure—the very fabric of our being. For Mezirow (1978), the experience is learning (as a process of constructing or reconstructing meaning) and is "intimately bound up with a person's growth and development" (Dirkx, 2012, p. 400), which Mezirow claims is unique to adulthood (Erickson, 2007, p. 66). This "adult hypothesis" has been tested in the study, as it is was not clear when or how the capacity for TL was developed before adulthood. It seems accepted as an adult skillset, yet it indeed does not appear full-orbed at age 18 or 21. So, what does it look like at earlier stages of life?

For Mezirow, every adult has a frame of reference or meaning perspective. This frame of reference contains two dimensions: (a) A habit of mind, and (b) a point of view. The habit of mind is a set of assumptions that are broad, generalized, orienting predispositions that act as filters for incoming experiences, thereby creating meaning. A "point of view is a set of immediate specific beliefs, feelings, attitudes, and value judgments" (Mezirow & Associates, 2000, p. 18). Mezirow claimed that points of view change more readily than habits of mind, mostly because of the feedback received about points of view. As a result, individuals are more likely to be aware of their own points of view (e.g., conscious of them) than they are habits of mind. By contrast, habits of mind may be more subconscious, or unconscious, based on our cultural upbringing or other experiences that have not been examined.

Mezirow's process, of which there are 10 progressive (and reiterative) steps, provides insight into and observation of an intensely private, internal process (see Table *1*).

Table 1

Mezirow's 10 Phases of Transformative Learning[1]

Phase	Description of the Phase of Transformative Learning
Phase 1	A disorienting dilemma
Phase 2	Self-examination with feelings of guilt or shame
Phase 3	A critical assessment of epistemic, sociocultural, or psychic assumptions
Phase 4	Recognition that one's discontent and the process of transformation are shared and that others have negotiated a similar change
Phase 5	Exploration of options for new roles, relationships, and actions
Phase 6	Planning a course of action
Phase 7	Acquisition of knowledge/skills for implementing one's plans
Phase 8	Provisional trying of new roles
Phase 9	Building competence and self-confidence in new roles and relationships
Phase 10	A reintegration into one's life on the basis of conditions dictated by one's new perspective

Mezirow & Associates (1991)

In defense of Mezirow, awareness of the 10 steps may help one transit the change with great alacrity. The question is, how many people are aware of the steps as they are going through

---

1 Reprinted with permission of John Wiley and Sons Inc according to the terms and conditions provided by John Wiley and Sons Inc and Copyright Clearance Center. License order # 4367690424177.

a transformative experience? How many want to slow down and follow a process? How might they flounder or get mixed up in the process? Can they do this automatically, or is this a learned process?

Dirkx (2012) refers to Mezirow's theory as a process of constructing and reconstructing meaning which is "intimately bound up with a person's growth and development" (p. 400). "[A]s we construct and reconstruct the meaning of our life experiences, we become more conscious," according to Dirkx (p. 400). It is possible that consciousness relates to the development of higher self-awareness, and through choices that relate to strengths and the risks of developing those strengths, possibly higher self-actualization. In essence, if we experience a number of significant trigger events that cause transformative learning to occur, is it possible that we develop some competence in changing ourselves and bouncing back faster?

Consciousness repeatedly appears throughout the literature as an essential construct in creating a motivation to change. For Kegan (1994), this consciousness-raising means becoming less subjected to or embedded in our thinking of whom we are, as well as becoming more open to questioning our habits of mind. As we do so, we become less embedded in unexamined, or unconscious, points of view and become willing to objectively test what we think we know and why we believe that we know it. Kegan (1994) has labeled this conscious/ unconscious mindset as a "subject-object orientation." This subject-object orientation is a significant diagnostic contribution for awareness of higher cognition and self-identification within higher levels of consciousness. In achieving these higher levels of thinking, individuals retain access to the earlier perspectives (and under severe stress might regress to them), but for the most part, adults evolve beyond the previous level and exist solely in the newer, higher level of consciousness.

Kegan (1994) presents this as a five-level model of meaning-making. These meaning-making schemas are also referred to in other writings as epistemologies (our approach to understanding of the world) and ontologies (consciousness of becoming). "Three of these levels are associated with the adult years" (Erickson, 2007, p. 64), and Kegan admits that few in general society evolve beyond his Level 3. While Mezirow illustrates his theory in a set of process steps by which he believes transformative change occurs, Kegan provides a stage-based theory for consciousness development. This model, and the practices Kegan has developed to enable conscious development, are in wide use globally. But what remains ignored in this approach is "a consideration of the same activity from the inside . . . from the point of view of the 'self,' when, what is at stake in preserving any given balance is the ultimate question of whether the 'self' shall continue to be, a naturally *onto*logical matter" (Kegan, 1982, p. 12).

"[T]he principles of mental organization are not only 'natural epistemologies' (subject-object structures found in nature), they are developmentally related to each other; each one is included in the next" (Kegan, 1994, p. 34). For further information on the Kegan levels, as well as a discussion about whether we can intervene and "incubate" the development of mental complexity, see *Immunity to Change*: How to Overcome it and Unlock Potential in Yourself and Your Organization, by R. Kegan and L. L. Lahey, pp. 21-30. Published 1997 by Harvard Business School.

Kegan makes the subjective objective by his subject-object model and through a set of practices subsumed within his "Immunity to Change" workshop, which grew out of his book by the same name (Kegan & Lahey, 2009). Kegan's subject-object tools scaffold the transformative changes one wishes to make, employing a deceptively provocative yet straightforward set of experiments to test our immunity (purposely employing a healthcare metaphor) to making changes in our lives. Similarly, Mezirow's prescription for perspective transformation can be marshaled as a self-diagnostic or coaching tool. These two theories and practices are both relevant and helpful in studying meaning making; they are by no means complete, but in combination offer new insights into the TL and identity change process. It could be suggested that Mezirow describes the process of transformation as it is unfolding, while Kegan's model describes the outcome of the unfoldment.

Poutiantine and Conners (2012) discuss the agreements in definition between Mezirow, Kegan, and Dirkx (2012) that "the disorienting dilemma represents a seed of new consciousness that can be either explored or ignored" (Poutiantine & Conners, p. 71). Poutiantine says the "[t]ransformative process can also be considered developmental as a cyclical process of identity formation and reformation" (p. 71). Individuals can recall the specific circumstances when they chose to respond to the dilemma, as Poutiantine discovered. The Poutiantine and Conners study participants recalled the specific circumstances when the choice to respond to a dilemma (in this case, when the individual decided to become a leader) occurred (p. 71). So, despite the "remarkable theoretical consistency" of Mezirow's contributions to adult learning theory, "[d]eveloping a conscious relationship with one's unconscious represents a central hallmark of a critical theory of self and of TL" (Dirkx, 2012, p. 399). The study of "individualistic perspectives helps us see how TL might represent a distinct form of adult learning" (p. 400).

Some of the more important themes of TL are found in the cognitive or psychocritical theories of Kegan (1994), Dirkx (2012), and Illeris (2014). Kegan (1994) and others would describe TL as "qualitative shifts in consciousness development" (p. 401), in which Dirkx includes consideration of our denial mechanisms and refusal to accept or even understand our "unconscious emotional conflicts that shape our behaviors" (p. 400). Through practices such as critical reflection and working through our immunity to change, both Mezirow and Kegan address how we can access and work on these less conscious influences (p. 403). While Dirkx has "focused on how unconscious emotional dynamics of individuals and groups can both facilitate and obstruct these meaning-making processes" (p. 400), Dirkx (2012) is more interested in the "complex processes of elaborating and remaking ways of understanding ourselves and our being in the world" (p. 400), which is referred to by many as *consciousness*. So, to study perspective transformation more comprehensively or holistically, the work of Dirkx (2012) and Illeris (2014) have been included in this literature review. Collectively, the "major theoretical approaches to TL . . . conceptualize experiences and [emphasis added] processes that fundamentally challenge some aspect of our being in the world, focusing on the complex processes associated with these dramatic shifts in consciousness and the sense of self emerging from them" (p. 400).

Criticisms of Transformative Learning Theory

There are many criticisms of each branch of TL theory, beginning with problems with Mezirow's study, which led researchers to "employ an analytic deduction strategy for engaging in qualitative inquiry and comparative case analysis that includes examining preconceived hypotheses," according to Patton (2002, p. 493). One of the most debated issues is that his "grounded theory study of women returning to college" is hard to replicate (Erickson, 2007, p. 68). Of all the criticisms, the most troubling is its overreliance on a North American context. Mezirow's study, for example, is evidence of a dominant, pale male, middle-class, North American perspective on the experience of women entering community college in adulthood. Merriam (2007) cites many questions about Mezirow's inattention to the power issues and social pressures that literally "wear us down" with the "sustained power of the normative ideology" (p. 150). The lack of attention to power dynamics was one of Brookfield's criticisms of Mezirow's narrow, overly rational orientation to TL (Illeris, 2014, p. 574). Daloz's criticism of Mezirow's notion that disorienting dilemmas are a single event is expressed by his comments on a study of the lives of 100 individuals:

[A]lthough a single event may catalyze a shift or a particular story might dramatize a transformation, closer examination reveals that change or shift was long in coming and its possibility prepared for in myriad ways, generally across years. (Daloz, 2000, p. 105)

Newman equates Daloz's insights as a developmental interpretation of TL. Dirkx (2012) supports Newman's criticism of Mezirow's apparent bias in not attending to the historical context of the Women's Liberation Movement. This was a valuable time for women, finding "newfound agency from the learning experience" (Newman, 2012, p. 39). Had Mezirow attended to this bias, it might have mitigated the question about whether the experiences of Mezirow's study participants could be attributed to a learning environment at all.

Another significant controversy about Mezirow falls into what Schapiro et al. describe as the "alone-together paradox. Mezirow and/or many readings of Mezirow privileged individual change while acknowledging that this change occurred within a social process" (Schapiro, Gallegos, Stashower, & Clark, 2017, p. 11), a primary tenet of emancipatory social change of adult educators of the day. "Most post-Jungian scholars present a postmodern perspective in which the 'self' is both multiplistic and unitary at the same time, in contrast to the critical or postmodern perspective which considers a core, unitary self as 'laughable'" (Dirkx, 2012, p. 403). So, it is possible that Mezirow was speaking of social emancipation as well as individualistic change that occurred within the social milieux of the women in his study and throughout his writings.

Since 2014, there has been a surge of interest in the transformative learning (TL) community, especially Mezirow (2000) and Dirkx (2012), in seeking a way to resolve the long-standing schisms in the definition of transformative learning. The Mezirow branch insists on a rational perspective that includes critical reflection and critical-dialectical discourse (Mezirow, 2003). The Dirkx followers, in depth psychology, include spirituality and the "depth transformation of the psyche" in their conceptual framework (Dix, 2016, p. 139). Hoggan (2016) has suggested 28 criteria to define and resolve the scholarly divisions by reclassifying TL as a meta-analytic theory, acknowledging that it most certainly has become one. At issue, are the (a) significant broadening of the definition of "learning" beyond a formal academic lens and, (b) a focus on identity development as the outcome of TL, or (c) even the possibility that transformative learning is the outcome of identity development.

Within this debate, Newman illuminates a vital point: "[T]ransformative learning theory fails to differentiate between identity and consciousness" (Newman, 2012, p. 394) stating that "identity is our persona, the self that we present to the world," while "consciousness . . . is the essence of our experience" (Newman, 2012, p. 394). This distinction is essential, since Mezirow's 10-step process is focused on the role consciousness plays in the outcome (i.e., the transformed consciousness) rather than the transformed identity. How to develop a transformed consciousness without it affecting one's identity once the unconscious becomes conscious is unclear, although it may become more evident through studies of individuals' life courses, as this study does. It will be one of the recurring themes of this research agenda to address a question at the intersection of TL and identity theory serving to answer the question: *What role does TL have in identity development?*

Illeris (2014) cites the history of the identity movement of the 1960s and 1970s as the motivating force for society's "unavoidable duty to create one's own life course and a significant personal profile" as well as the "liberation to increased competition in work education and consumption" (p. 578). The responsibility of choice puts demands on individuals. A failure to satisfy this duty successfully becomes a source of great distress. It has become a cultural script to be able to fulfill one's life dreams.

As to where these cultural scripts come from, a significant contribution by Habermas and Bluck (2000) describes the influence these cultural scripts can have on a person's consciousness and identity as early as childhood. Suffice it to say, children are encoded with culturally expected life events at an early age. It is likely that failure to achieve these societal expectations can be a source of transformative dilemmas in adulthood, as well as emotional disorders or the inability "to realize their true individuality" (King & Nicol, 1999, p. 236). An example for those in the developed world would be the dilemmas of foregoing marriage or childbirth and parenting to advance one's career.

There are "five main themes of intersections between various theories and disciplines" of TL and practice as it has evolved since 1978 (Schapiro, Gallegos, Stashower, & Clark, 2017, p. 19). The TL community is now at a crossroads with many challenges to Mezirow's requirement of discourse for "legitimate" TL in the face of the deeply personal and meaningful work of the intrapersonal and physical demands of living in a world that makes no sense to us. Moreover, TL is being expanded "through its intersection with other ways of thinking about transformation and development, as expressed in other theories and disciplines . . . [including] . . . constructive developmental theory . . . and identity formation" (p. 8). Transformative learning describes the "role of different kinds of meaning making; about the dialogue between the subconscious and the conscious mind through our dreams and our art; . . . about inner spiritual space, our senses, and our construction of reality . . . changes [that] must be integrated into our whole self if they are to impact fully our ways of being and our ways of knowing" (p. 9). Inherent in the work of those in a transformative teaching or coaching role is the element of providing safe "containers that provide both the safety and the provocation that leads people to take risks, leave their comfort zones, and engage in the kind of collaborative inquiry that can lead to TL" (p. 10).

Throughout 2007-2017, two vital theoretical issues in TL have been disturbing:

1.   Why does TL apply only to adults?

How does TL develop, if not learned in earlier life? How does one acquire and cultivate the tools or experiences that set up a TL moment? What is it, then, that is different across childhood, adolescence, and adulthood that could be represented as TL? To this first point, whether TL is legitimately just an "adult learning" theory, Illeris (2015) questions "where the ability to make such transformations come from, how and when does it start, and at which age can we be regarded as adults" (p. 580)? He specifically states that "finding out how this takes place would be an important contribution to the understanding and practice of TL," which is the intention of this study (p. 580).

2.   What is different about TL and identity?

Isn't the point of TL to integrate new perspective into our identity, our ontology, or who I am? If not, why not? If it is true, how would it be experienced and described? What does it tell us about how authentic the TL was? How do we become aware of who we are or who we are becoming? Illeris suggests that "linking TL to identity opens up significant new possibilities" (p. 580). This could mean that TL may be the process of identity development, and identity is the outcome. This is a vital component of this study's research question.

The field of TL is in a philosophical quandary at present: Do we or do we not have a legitimate theory? Hoggan (2016) offers a way to resolve the discord and allow scholars to find congruence (i.e., consenting that TL is a meta-analytical framework). Hoggan's way is to embrace the intersections, the theories, and the disciplines by creating a unified coding system or typology that allows various points of view to coalesce despite their discrepancies. The conception of self-directed identity formation may lay the foundational processes that are further carried into adulthood with TL. In other words, TL may be an extension of Erikson's theory. "In general, it seems evident that the connection of TL to identity and its development and formation can be strongly conducive to how, when and why TL starts and is developed through childhood and youth" (Illeris, 2015, p. 581).

The Link Between Transformative Learning and Identity

The conceptualization of the self is related to Jung's (1933, 1957) theory of individuation in the search for soul and self-knowledge, through which we create ourselves through interactions with others. The evolution of this theory of individuation can be traced throughout the history of TL. An example is by comparison of identity and consciousness to Jung's "individuation," Mezirow's (1981, 1991) "perspective transformation," and Freire's (1999) "conscientization." The role of consciousness in learning is accepted, but the definition of consciousness separate from identity has not been clear. This study examines the role of consciousness while trying to see how identity is involved. Narrative identity researchers believe that *identity is a life story*. This *story*, in contemporary Western society, puts demands on individuals to be our own "protagonist in a lifelong journey, marked by the mutual challenges of intimacy and autonomy, expressed through archetypal characters, turning points, and varying outcomes of redemption or contamination" (Singer, 2004, p. 445).

A fundamental question throughout the TL literature between 2007 and 2017 has been whether identity really *is* transformative learning. This study will rely predominantly on Erickson's (2007) framework for identity which takes into consideration the concept of continuity, or the persistence of an individual's identity, over the lifespan even while the system of meaning construction is evolving. This idea, in which the core self—the idiosyncrasies that separate one person from another—endures through a lifetime and is formed through stages. The sense that "identity is formed in response to challenges and human interaction" (Karp & Helgo, 2009) includes individual cognition, and it may include the strategies an individual uses to adapt to his or her socially constructed and cultural world. As confirmed by the Karp and Helgo (2009) study, the self is a social construction, not based exclusively on an individual's estimation of him or herself. The "self "is being created and re-created, and it is therefore important to be "seen" by others in the process. Karp and Helgo (2009) describe identity as a "movement in time and space constituting a collection of self-images in our mind from the past (Jung's *Grounded Self*), from the present (Jung's *True Self*), which [form] the future (Jung's *Possible Self*), all results of human interaction" (p. 887).

By 2017, identity has become the new lens for examining TL. For purposes of this study, the perspective transformation under investigation is identity. "Identity, as used throughout the social sciences, is an individual's comprehension of himself or herself as a discrete, separate entity" (Karp & Helgo, 2009, p. 880). As defined within psychology, identity often relates to self-image, self-esteem, personality, and individuation (Karp & Helgo, 2009). Newman (2012) suggested that individuals become skilled at adapting or changing their identities at an early age, and therefore, the hypothesis that an identity-development capability is developed before adulthood can be acknowledged.

In his "Mutinous Thoughts" treatise on transformative learning, Newman (2012) draws a distinction between identity and consciousness with this definition:

Identity is the more superficial of the two. It is the face, the mask, the person we present to the world. . . . Identity manifests itself in our actions, the context and companions we choose, our physical appearance, and the objects we gather around us. It is an aspect of the self that we can deal with rationally; and from an early age on we become adept at adjusting and even changing it significantly. (p. 42)

Newman (2012) further states that "consciousness is a project in the making from our earliest days until our death. It becomes the medium through which we apprehend the self and give meaning to the world the self inhabits. In this sense, consciousness is a relationship between entities, and not an entity in and of itself. Moreover, in another sense, consciousness is all-encompassing, infinite. It is literally all we have, and with it neither the self nor the world exists" (p. 42). Newman furthers his position that consciousness-raising is an internal, individualized experience using Daloz's (2000) description of "perspective transformation . . . as an individual, even lonely experience (p. 105), and by this connection cements the point that *perspective transformation is the result of a change in consciousness* and it forms our identity from the "inside" out. Newman (2012) describes TL as "reworking our identity . . . tinker[ing] with our being" (p. 42). Newman proposes that effective learning contributes to the continuing creation of our consciousness.

"There is no doubt that the terms 'self' and 'identity' are the most generally used to indicate the individual's mental totality" (Illeris, 2015, p. 576). Illeris has proposed that when we consider the terms "identity" and "self," experts on adult learning (Tennant, in this case) are referring to the "self" as an entirely psychological concept and refer to the self as the *mental instance* to which TL is related. In other words, transformative learning interacts with the conscious self. For this exact reason, Illeris proposes that TL employs the term "identity" because the social dimension and sociological insights are crucial to a full understanding of TL. Going further, Illeris (2015) proposes this new definition of TL:

The concept of transformative learning comprises all learning which implies changes in the identity of the learner. (p. 577)

This definition combines the terms of individuality and sociality under one umbrella definition of TL that embraces the concept of identity. Illeris returns us to our modern understanding of identity. In Illeris' writing, he takes the position of the "psycho-social" conceptualization of identity. To quote Illeris (2015), "covering both the internal personal experience of being the same in all the different situations of life, and the totality of how we relate to, and wish to be perceived by others. This double-sided identity was, according to Erikson, mainly developed during youth and maintained as a core of the personality for the rest of life" (Illeris, 2015).

How Identity Theory Evolved with TL

The 1960s and '70s, were the beginning of the "Me Generation." During this time, it became apparent that the concept of a *stable* identity could no longer be sustained, at least not within the United States. The responsibility of dealing with all the possibilities that this society affords and expects puts pressure on individuals to transform elements of themselves to keep pace with social changes and expectations. It is this *urge* to manage ourselves, to take advantage of the opportunities and expectations in our society, which creates the case for TL as an important way to manage this tension. In fact, according to Illeris (2015), the early '70s, especially in the United States, is

when identity began to be questioned, originally because classic neurotic symptoms in psychotherapy gradually seemed to be replaced by a new type of personality problems, including feelings of lack of self-perception, emptiness, lack of job satisfaction and initiative, absurdity, and an increased tendency towards routine behavior—altogether described as "narcissist disorders" or "pathological behavior"—by the American psychoanalysts Kohut (1971, 1977) and Kernberg (1975). (pp. 577-78)

Turning our attention to psychology and psychoanalysis, some psychologists have broken from the medical or clinical view of psychology, which takes a pathological lens, and have begun to approach identity through a personality lens. A noted psychologist in this vein, McAdams, sees personality as constituting a pattern of *situational* behaviors, which are more akin to Newman's description of the face or the mask that we present to the world. McAdams claims that there is an 'I' who seeks to become a 'Me', where the 'Me' is the end product and the 'I' [is] the reflective process" (Karp & Helgo, 2009, p. 887). Note how similarly Kegan, McAdams, Newman, and Illeris describe the phenomenon of identity.

For this study, a contrast and comparison of the cognitive, developmental theorists (Mezirow and Kegan), with a view into the emotional and spiritual realms of the theory (Dirkx and Illeris) contribute and enrich the most interesting intersections of these related theories to situate the phenomenon of interest for this study—identity development through TL. This study claims that developmental learning is linked to meaning construction in foreseeable ways throughout the lifespan. Evidence in the life story narratives of the study subjects proves or disproves this claim.

Narrative identity, a new subdiscipline in personality psychology, identifies how people use their story to develop and hold onto a sense of personal identity and purpose from experiences throughout all stages of their lives. Linking the TL literature with identity theory, we turn to McAdams. His theory "asserts that people living in modern societies provide their lives with unity and purpose by constructing internalized and evolving narratives of the self" (McAdams, 2001).

As a personality psychologist, McAdams approaches identity through the lens of personality. McAdams developed a specific interview protocol for a life story interview to understand the role of identity in the personality. What is essential to leadership research and development of the personality of an individual leader is not just the description of the role the leader plays, nor the behavior of the individual leader and the reactions of followers and other stakeholders to that leader, but the underlying narrative the leader has about who he/she is in the world. Understanding this level of the individual's interpretation of being a leader through his/her narrative lens can be enormously revealing not only for that individual with a "strong power motivation" and sense of agency as a leader, but for those seeking to achieve higher levels of self-mastery, status, and responsibility (McAdams, 2001). This study charts that process. This study serves the calls for research into TL *as* identity. The varied ways to achieve this through a semi-structured interview is widely appealing, and the McAdams interview protocol (1995) affords a legitimacy of data across the narrative psychology, TL, and leadership literatures.

Employing McAdams' life story interview method (1995) to collect the data for this study served to bracket the evidence of TL experiences with dense, personally revealing descriptions of life experiences. The narratives uncovered the antecedents as well as projected futures of TL due to the autobiographic detail of the subjects' experiences. The McAdams' frame of reference on consciousness and identity fit well with the TL criticisms of Newman and supports Illeris's definition of identity. To rephrase Karp and Helgo (2009), the "I" (the conscious and unconscious I) who seeks to become a "Me" (my personality, that me which can adapt socially) where the "Me" is the end product (that I choose to show to the world) and the "I" [is] the reflective process (inside of me, my consciousness). The narrative lens is the preferred method for developing insight into these phenomena.

It is potentially bothersome to the psychologists that narrative interview methods lack an organizing principle (other than time), and that the descriptions provided may be focused on the "cognitive and conscious aspects of personality at the expense of the irrational, affective, and unconscious factors that shape individuals and their behavior" (Singer, 2004, p. 440). Since the "narrative memories . . . [are an account] of the individual's goal pursuits, obstacles, and outcomes (Singer, p. 441), it is interesting to note that this storyline is embedded in a schema and an actual script that describes the event within a living story, giving it both historicity and meaning. It is also intriguing that the storyline may change, upon reflection on experience.

Adding to the complexity of a new science (of personality), the "scripted units" of the personality within the life story are given different names, including McAdams (1985) "nuclear episodes," or Phillemer's (1998) "memorable events," or Singer's (1995) "self-defining memories," or Bluck and Gluck's (2004) "autobiographical memory narratives" (Singer, 2004, p. 441). As Bohn and Berntsen (2008) uncovered in their research of Danish children, the storyline of a basic script follows a culturally-expected life which becomes the organizing principle for most stories (p. 1143). Also, of note is the age at which the random events in life take on significance sufficient to become an actual story, rather than an odd assortment of "and this happened."

Developmental psychologists believe that orienting predispositions (like Mezirow's "habits of mind") act as filters for experiences throughout life. Generalized meaning schemas are provided by our culture (Habermas & Bluck, 2000). The drive to become and to have a more complete sense of self often exposes people to experiences that cannot be accommodated in their existing meaning schemas, which may trigger transformation. These experiences are variously called dialectical thinking (Erikson), provocative learning (McAdams), disorienting dilemmas (Mezirow), part of the five phases of critical thinking (Brookfield), or disjuncture (Jarvis). As an individual enters this "trigger experience," internal changes in consciousness may occur. According to developmental psychologists Mezirow and Kegan, these trigger experiences change a person's meaning-making perspective(s). If these conscious triggers are robust enough to disrupt the unconscious, if they run counter to accepted general meaning schemas (see Habermas and Bohn), and if they are also contrary to the sense of self, an immediate and sudden realization can occur which Mezirow (2000) refers to as an epiphany. Importantly, for the epiphany to be complete requires three ingredients: (a) to think about the experience, (b) to process ways to deal with the experience, and (c) to examine long-held assumptions or premises about the situation. *If reflection also occurs, according to Mezirow (2000), TL is the result* (p. 18).

Leadership Theory

For those in leadership roles, transformative learning and identity development evolve over time depositing an individual into a life flow that usually includes questions about who they are as leaders. While many adults would express that their career choices were less than planful, some individuals feel called to certain types of leadership roles. This study is focused on those called to career duties that include leading far-flung operations in different countries and defining themselves within that role. We will learn more about why certain individuals find these roles personally desirable, while others may find them quite tricky. In either case, for purposes of this study, the definitions of *global*, *senior*, and *leader* are relevant to the contributions this study can make to the literature. Each term will be defined here.

Definition of the Global Leader

For most of the early 2000s, the role of a global leader was primarily defined by the description of a *role* that had international in the title, had different responsibilities from leaders operating solely in a domestic market, were often changing, and required long-distance travel.

Much more precisely, the term *global* is defined by the differentiators in the *tasks* that global leaders execute, empirically tested by Caligiuri (2006, p. 220) in her study on developing global leaders:

Tasks of Global Leaders

1. Global leaders work with colleagues from other countries.
2. Global leaders interact with external clients from other countries.
3. Global leaders interact with internal clients from other countries.
4. Global leaders may need to speak in a language other than their mother tongue at work.
5. Global leaders supervise employees who are of different nationalities.

6. Global leaders develop a strategic business plan on a worldwide basis for their unit.

7. Global leaders manage a budget on a worldwide basis for their unit.

8. Global leaders negotiate in other countries or with people from other countries.

9. Global leaders manage foreign suppliers or vendors.

10. Global leaders manage risk on a worldwide basis for their unit.

(Caligiuri, 2006, p. 220)

Definition of global leadership. The purpose of setting this study in the global leadership domain within the international management and leadership literature is to illuminate how intercultural and cognitive abilities develop over time (Osland et al., 2007). "After conducting an extensive review of literature, Joyce Osland concluded that effectiveness and selection criteria have received little attention" (Holt & Seki, 2012, p. 198). This study provides a small contribution of criteria to fit this need.

It appears that an active link exists between leadership context and identity (Gagnon, 2014) that undergirds the emergence and exercise of leadership and, with it, identity development dynamics. This study posits that the global leader's identity is made more congruent through transformative learning in a global leadership role. The global leader role contributes to the ongoing feedback loop available to support a virtuous cycle of confronting points of view dynamically on a frequent and regular basis while working with different cultures across different geographies. It is these cross-cultural experiences that contribute to the improvement of a leader's capacity to manage successfully, at least as defined by measures of global leadership success (Tucker et al., 2014).

For the first decade of the 21st century, theories and models of global leadership began to identify the many capabilities needed for success. Scholars including Javidan, Mendenhall, Osland, Bird, Beechler, and Baltzley provided ample evidence of precisely how competencies for success are different when viewed on a global scale. As crucial as this definitional work has been, global scholars have yet to identify the *antecedents* in the development of the cognitive and emotional capacity that is so crucial to this global work. The identification and description of these *antecedents* is one contribution of this study. A gap also exists in studying the life history of adult leaders who perform global leadership roles in multinational organizations. This study contributes life story narratives to address this gap. At the same time, this study addresses a question at the intersection of TL and identity theory with research serving to answer the question: "What role does TL have on identity development?" A hunch is that studying the life experiences of global general managers will provide a longitudinal description of the meaning these executives have made of experiences across their lifespans. It may also provide exposure to what accounts for their unusual ability and capacity to withstand complex, demanding, challenging, ambiguous experiences with multinational decisions, people, and processes in the organization. This study examines whether they had significant, transformative events across their lifetimes and if they did, how that may have affected the trajectory of their expected life course in their native cultures.

Description of the global organizational context. In the 21st century, "the global environment has not only changed the way [business] is conducted; it has also changed the criteria of effectiveness for the firm's leaders in the way business is conducted" (Caligiuri & Tarique, 2009, p. 336). As companies solidified cross-border trade agreements and figured out the complex financial and tax structures of deals made possible with changing tax laws and the easing of trade policies, more organizations began to import and export people to remain competitive in these developing markets. All Fortune 500 companies have interactions across their ecosystems and must be able to manage them differently. These organizations decided that, as good as they were and could be, they needed to change to get to the next level. This organizational transformation drives the need for leaders who can transform right along with these organizational changes. This organizational shift impacts on the identity of work, and the identity of the worker is personal.

With a geographically dispersed operating team structure, it has become essential to manage cross-cultural communications, labor/management issues, and to harmonize employee benefits across different country borders, especially since organizations have become aware of the advantages of doing so. "Given the strategic importance of their tasks, successful global leaders are a competitive advantage for multinational firms" (Caligiuri, 2006, p. 219). "Stroh and Caligiuri (1998a) found that developing leadership cross-cultural competence was among the top 5 organization-wide practices affecting the effectiveness of multinational corporations" (Caligiuri, 2006, p. 219).

What is a global leader (GL) for the 21st century exactly? Is this a set of tasks, a role, or a leadership style? Are there specific traits for this work? McCall and Hollenbeck (2002) have been cited in numerous studies of global leadership capabilities. Heams and Harvey (2006) produced a 70-year study of the leadership literature to identify the "20th Century Leader" defined by Chester Barnard (1948) to the "21st Century Leader" defined by McCall and Hollenbeck (2002). For purposes of this study, the 21st Century leader is referred to as "the global leader." Table 2 compares the two side by side:

Table 2

A Comparative View of the 20th Century Manager with the 21st Century Global Leader[2]

20th Century Manager (early 1900s)	21st Century Global Leader (early 2000's)
1. Broad interests & wide imagination and understanding	1. Open minded & flexible
2. Superior intellectual capabilities	2. Value-added technical & business skills
3. Understanding of the field of human relations	3. Cultural interest & sensitivity
4. Appreciate the importance of persuasion in human affairs	4. Resilient, resourceful, optimistic, & energetic
5. Understand what constitutes rational behavior toward the unknown & the unknowable	5. Able to deal with complexity
	6. Stable personal life
	7. Possess and engender honesty and integrity

(Barnard, 1948, pp. 195-204 and McCall & Hollenbeck, 2002, p. 35 in Heams & Harvey, 2006, p. 36)

---

2 Note: Permission is granted to republish or display content in this dissertation from the publisher, Pergamon, and the Rightsholder, Elsevier Science & Technology Journals. Confirmation number 11723590.

The differences between the 20th and 21st century leader are profound. The transformation, as shown in Table 2, set a new era for intra- and inter-organizational dynamics. What are the shifts or pivots that are required individually and organizationally to help leaders learn how people are different, and moreover, how all around the world, people are different?

The mental complexity required to operate in this transformed world is illustrated by the work of Elliott Jaques. Jaques's framework for potential capacity (PC) describes how "at any given stage in life, individuals possess a mental capacity that determines their PC to handle a certain level of complexity" (King & Nicol, 1999, p. 239). An organization can and often does determine the potential capacity of the individual to more effectively align "individuals and their roles" (p. 239), and the fact that the executive is operating at this level suggests his/ her PC for complexity. It is precisely the capacity to lead in this challenging, new environment that serves this study well.

Transitioning from the 20th to the 21st century, what do we need to learn about how we think of ourselves, how we behave, and how we lead? How do we learn to behave in new ways and help people become skillful in transparent and high-integrity settings? This is the context this study's research question is cast in. Further, we need to prepare ourselves for the forecasted changes in global leadership requirements anticipated as we look to 2030. In answer to these questions, and to a call to the HRD community, we need global leadership skills at all levels of the organization (Cumberland, Herd, Alagaraja, & Kerrick, 2016, p. 302). This organizational context is the setting for the study being undertaken in this instance and it is the importance of this study to serve the needs of this transforming organizational landscape. It is not just theoretical; therefore, it is pragmatic to understand how individuals develop their global identity as leaders in service to the institutions that they serve.

How are global leaders developed? McCall and Hollenbeck (2002) still the primary source for definitions across the literature, defining global leaders as "those who do global work." Mendenhall et al.'s work supports a redefinition to include "individuals who effect significant positive change in organizations by building communities through the development of trust and the arrangement of organizational structures and processes in a context involving multiple cross-boundary stakeholders, multiple sources of external cross-boundary authority, and multiple cultures under conditions of temporal, geographic and cultural complexity" (Mendenhall et al. 2008, p. 17). So, some combination of relationship skills and task capabilities is required to be a successful global leader.

In 2010, IBM conducted a study of global chief human resource officers to determine the most essential business skills for the future. As found by Heams and Harvey (2006), "the changes that occurred in the marketplace over the past 70 plus years are exceptional and represent significant shifts in the way executives run global hypercompetitive enterprises" (p. 39). The results of the IBM study were revealing. (See also "Capitalizing on Complexity: Insights from the 2011 Global Chief Executive Officer Study," IBM Institute for Business Values, Armonk, NY). According to Cumberland et al. (2016), "developing future leaders" was the most important business skill needed to achieve business objectives (p. 302). In the same IBM study, the "workforce gaps which needed to be addressed included hiring, developing and retaining what the Human Resource officers called 'borderless leaders' who could function effectively in complex global environments and manage global business teams" (p. 302). However, knowing that a gap exists and doing something about fixing that gap are two different things.

According to Osland et al. (2007), global leadership skills apparently develop along a learning path that includes specialized knowledge, skills, and abilities, including a highly developed tolerance for "managing complexity" (Osland et al., 2007). Linking TL as defined by Kegan (1994) to the development of GL as defined by Osland et al., we can see that Kegan's stage theories suggest levels of intercultural competencies (worldview, social interpersonal style, and situational approach) and cognitive abilities (personality and motives) that develop over time (Kegan, p. 352). Cumberland et al. offered this description of what GL competence is: "GL leadership competencies encompass personality traits, knowledge, and skills, as well as behaviors" (Cumberland et al., 2016, p. 301).

In practice, even by 2017, there is still a significant amount of confusion over whether global leaders should be selected based on a personality profile or developed based on a set of competencies which include knowledge, skills, and abilities. It is likely that the answer is "yes," yet this gap remains. Cumberland et al. (2016) propose that "effective assessment practices" are the answer to identify, select, and develop the prospective global talent in an organization.

Identifying those with the potential for success as a global leader. The next problem is identifying an appropriate assessment tool that captures most of the global personality traits, dispositions, knowledge, and skills that form the core building blocks of success. There were 17 such assessments at the time of publication of Cumberland et al.'s article. In 2016, the newest psychometric entrant into this crowded field was released by Tucker International. In response to the demand in the market, and perhaps the call from Marquardt and Berge, Tucker et al. (2014) conducted a study with a representative sample comprised exclusively of global leaders to meet three specific research requirements:

1. To develop a concise set of intercultural competencies and a separate set of global leadership success factors with excellent psychometric properties that can be used to compare among leaders of different nationalities.

2. The need to validate intercultural competencies against separate criteria of global leadership success.

3. The need to detect social desirability or "fake good" responses in self-response instruments and make appropriate corrections.

The result of the Tucker et al. research was a 107-item psychometrically sound tool (GLTAP) that assesses nine intercultural competencies, and nine items testing social desirability of the respondent's answers, or "faking good" items. The instrument uses a 5-point, Likert-type scale. Fifty-nine of the study participants were top executives, 51% had profit and loss responsibilities, 50% had responsibility over a group of businesses, and 42% had senior executive responsibility for their business function. The resulting global leader model to which the assessment maps includes the distal attributes, the proximal attributes, and the leadership criteria for success. It represents a remarkable improvement over previous tools and is represented in

Table *3*. The Tucker et al. framework provides significant direction for this study.

Table 3

The GLTAP Assessment Framework

Category	Level of Analysis	Competencies
Distal[3] Attributes	Cognitive, personality, and motive attributes	
Proximal[4] Attributes	Competencies	Instilling Trust Adapting Socially Respecting Beliefs Navigating Ambiguity Even Disposition Demonstrating Creativity
Leadership Criteria for Success	Business Environment Processes Success Area Leader Advancement Model	

(Tucker, Bonial, Vandhove, & Kedharnath, 2014, p. 18; adapted from Zacarro, 2017[5]).

The Study of Global Leaders in Their Organizational Setting

This study adopts the *senior* leader definition from Caligiuri which is, "high level professionals such as executives, vice presidents, directors, and managers." The term *global* is defined as those "who are in jobs with some global leadership

---

[3] The term distal as used in this instance refers to the more (or most) distant of two or more things, in the sense that these dimensions or attributes of global leaders are intrinsic, stable, and more dissimilar to each other. They are discrete concepts and are a priori, hence based on theoretical deduction rather than empirical observation

[4] The term proximal as used in this instance refers to the central point or the point of view that describes similar factors or those attributes that can be observed, developed, or not stable.

[5] Reprinted with permission of the authors and publisher.

activities such as global integration responsibilities" (Caligiuri & Tarique, 2009, p. 336) and embodies the 2008 Mendenhall et al. definition. As described previously, the 10 tasks of global leaders provided by the Caligiuri work will be a significant scale for selection in this study.

Finding a tool to consistently define and measure effectiveness and achieve agreement on what constitues success for leaders is a more difficult task, mainly because leaders are often selected for global roles primarily based on their technical capabilities. To overcome this challenge in this study, the Global Business Experience (GBE) measure (Tucker et al., 2014), a 12-item questionnaire with a 20-point rating scale was selected. The GBE measures three factors: Global networking, driving performance, and building team effectiveness. Tucker et al, (2014) reported that overall GBE scores (the Success Index) and each of the three GBE factors were represented and provided support for the hypothesis that the "extracted criterion factors will assess the level of success among global leaders" (Tucker et al., 2014, p. 6). The Tucker et al. (2014) validation study was conducted with nine nationalities consisting of 689 leaders. As already discussed, this species of leadership theory offers ties to transformative learning and identity due to the organizational context for *this* type of leader.

The Link Between Global Leadership and Identity

There are more than 50 different ways personality traits can be defined, but almost never included are the overlapping constructs of knowledge, skills, abilities, and outcomes (Jokinen, 2005). A rich literature has developed linking leadership context with identity (Gagnon, 2014). While the terminology used to describe global leaders is often consistent, it is unclear whether core personality traits (e.g., openness to learning, being hardy) are essential to success. What is clear from research by Petriglieri and Stein is that "identity dynamics" undergird the "emergence and exercise of leadership" because "leaders are meaning makers." It is also clear that most Western countries preference *doing* over *being*. Holt and Seki reported that throughout the leadership development literature, even discussions or tips on developing "self-knowledge" do not speak to the issue of *being* (Heams & Harvey, 2006, p. 207). In essence, global leaders are being developed based on a model with tendencies toward tasks, actions, and decision making rather than how to "help people discover and engage their natural energy to improve the quality of their *being* [sic]" (p. 207). It seems relevant to the development of global leaders to create the link between *being* and their identity, since leaders need to develop and maintain a leader identity especially when working across cultures.

Leader identity work involves creating a congruence between their authentic selves and their leader selves (i.e., leader identity). Alternative definitions of leadership that are in general use within the business community, and of late are gaining increased attention from leadership scholars, are theories of the authenticity of a leader. This has a general appeal as a corollary to identity theory. The authentic leader learns to wear a mask and consciously evolve in order to become more transparent as experiences provoke self-reflection leading to more significant self-awareness, curiosity, humility, and openness to express who one is (i.e., one's identity), as compared to how one wishes to be perceived. This growth process may be described along a continuum from "faking it" to "fully authentic." So, it stands to reason that leaders are most effective when their message is intensely personal (i.e., authentic) and touches the shared concerns of their constituents. A leader's ability to claim a leader identity that is successful is contingent on being congruent with his/her life story. Employees can tell if a leader telling a story about himself/herself is incongruent with the employees' experience of the leader's behavior, for example.

This personal assessment for change is a large part of the work global leaders must undertake to understand themselves, define their ontology, and convert it into a deontology. That is, creating a personal leadership theory that defines their personal philosophy of leading. This deontology presents a set of boundary conditions or moral considerations that the leader can use to determine whether the action he or she is taking as a leader is right or wrong. It offers a leader a set of rules to live by rather than acting purely from a commercial point of view, and it is intensely personal.

How does a leader examine the unwanted aspects of himself/herself to craft an authentic leadership identity? In their influential article, "The Unwanted Self: Projective Identification in Leaders' Identity Work," Petriglieri and Stein (2012) provide an explicit model that leaders can use to examine the wanted and unwanted aspects of themselves and then craft their ideal leadership identity. A visualization of this model, adapted from the Petriglieri and Stein work, may be helpful in self-assessment and development of the global leader. This model is offered in Figure 1.

	Conscious (Have)		
	Natural	*Develop Awareness/ Mitigate*	
Wanted/ Desirable	*Raise Awareness; Be More Integrated*	*Become Aware of How Dysfunction Shows Up*	<u>Unwanted/ Undesirable</u>
	Unconscious (Do Not Have; Hope I Do Not Have)		

Figure 1. A depiction of Petriglieri & Stein's[6] Leader Identity Assessment. (Adapted from Petriglieri and Stein, 2012)

Leadership in the Context of Commercial Requirements

Up to this point, the literature discussion points to the journey inside the leader. Leadership operates in context. A leader is confronted with different situations in which to lead. Does the leader's behavior drive business success as well, and if so, how do we construct a view of that leader who rapidly adapts or rises to a new level in the actions taken (i.e., the "outside" demonstration of their "inside" thinking) in the world of work? How do we measure success using context as a framework?

Bazigos, Gagnon, and Schaniger (2016) offer a view of leadership in context, a revisiting of the Blanchard model of situational leadership, applying the health of the company as the measure of the *situation*. In distinctly rational and objective terms, the leadership behaviors identified in Bazigos et al.'s empirical work (2016, p. 5) suggests that six specific behaviors are required for maintaining a top-tier level of performance, which they describe as "successful." These behaviors fit into

---

[6] Note: Permission is grated for the life of this dissertation on a non-exclusive basis, in the English language, throughout the world in all formats provided full citation is made to the original SAGE publication.

two different classifications: The first is the baseline, which is essential in any situation; and the situational, which is related to the current "health" measurement of the corporation. The baseline is the essential business level of leadership. One might say, the foundation is the least expectation for a leader's behavior.

These two measures model the leadership exemplars from a survey of greater than 375,000 people from 165 organizations in multiple industries and geographies. This short checklist of behaviors is defined in two types: (a) a baseline set of behaviors that are considered *tablestakes*, or the entry fee for leadership, and (b) situational behaviors that are required for motivating a team (individually and collectively) and an ability to reflect the values of the organization (p. 5). This description of 21st century leadership in action suggests that the deontology of the leader must broadly consider both essential and situational variables. The successful leader is held to these basic standards of behavior, and the outside world measures them according to their ability to meet these criteria. A leader must develop these behaviors to confront the challenges of the day.

One of the more significant challenges is how a senior leader continues his/her development of leadership skills and behaviors and adapts his/her deontology as the organizational situation shifts. Henderson claims that "studies that identify the importance of learning for executive performance and success focus on development of managers and executives, not on the development of CEOs (Bennis & Nanus, 1985, Bray et al., 1974, Dechant, 1990; Hall, 1986; Kaplan, Drath, & Kofodimos, 1987; Kets de Vries, 1989a; Kolb, 1976, Kotter, 1995; Lombardo & Eichinger, 1997; McCall & Lombardo, 1983;

McCall et al., 1988; Yukl, 1994)" (Henderson, 2002, p. 11). As previously discussed, for transformative learning to occur the context of learning is critical (Henderson, 2002). For this study, it is essential to differentiate the *context* of learning for a senior global executive to determine whether seniority (such as board-level situations), physical location, or other context variables have particular significance to changes in meaning-making that could be triggered. This *context* for learning is just not adequately understood. This study will explore in which types of situations or circumstances a senior leader found the time for reflection and which types of scenarios trigger those reflective and possibly transformative experiences. In today's advanced technological environment, social media, cell phones, and other communication vehicles (Facebook, email, Twitter, etc.) are included in a broad description of situations in which leaders find themselves and which could create TL sufficient to shift identity.

Summary and Working Conceptual Framework for the Study

The literature review provided three specific yet interrelated concepts. TL provided views into the enduring, natural, and organic process of how our perspective transforms as we experience profound questions (or become conscious) about who we are (self-awareness/identity) and how we want to show up in the world (persona or social identity). As we experience this consciousness-raising, we make new meaning of our experiences (life stories). This study seeks to understand the capacity or disposition of global leaders to learn from their experiences (identity of global leaders).

As there is no universal learning theory nor a single TL theory, this study has chosen to focus attention on perspective transformation as the closest parallel phenomenon that calls TL into view within the context of the leaders' life stories. Beginning with the end in mind, the question for this study is how leaders develop the capacity for handling complex, paradoxical situations that involve reading and interpreting people, economics, complex financial data, and making sense out of all of it so that decisions can be made under uncertainty in volatile, uncertain, complex, and ambiguous business conditions while mitigating private compulsions, obsessions, and more unconscious matters that might drive decision making. The research question also seeks answers to *when* they begin developing that capacity.

According to Singer (2004), the researchers who place "narrative identity at the center of personality" draw on three measures of personality: "Traits, such as the Big Five, and Level 2 "Characteristic Adaptations" constructs, such as personal strivings or motives, but their primary emphasis is on Level 3 "Identity and Life Stories" (pp. 437-438). Identity researchers are engaged in a humanistic concern in the meaning making, spiritual depth, and self-understanding as "defined by life stage, gender, ethnicity, class, and culture" (Singer, p. 438). TL theorists are concerned with the same phenomena. "This sensitivity to the nuances of sociocultural context prevents the privileging of a dominant ideological position, masquerading as an 'objective' scientific principle" (Singer, p. 439). It is precisely the notion that *learning* engages the consciousness with no discernible ending nor beginning that suggests a life history interview method would illuminate when and how a change in perspective might have occurred, and to trace the change in identity, or evolving consciousness of becoming, which may be documented in the narrative of the life story interview. This study contributes value to each literature.

As suggested by Turner and Mavin (2008), further research is needed about the experience of isolation and vulnerability as well as how emotions impact the performance of leaders in their roles. This study looks to life story narrative to see what and how emotions show up in the leader's story. Few studies look at the transformative life experiences of senior executives' lives through the lens of identity, primarily as it was defined by Dirkx (2012).

It is the very nature of life experiences, particularly emotionally charged experiences, to create a psychic tear in the timeline and perspective. What once may have been a physically painful or sickening feeling is replaced with a new realization that the incident was just a part of life, perhaps a growing up or growing through a particular experience. The pain has subsided, and the outlook shifts from the past hurt to the learnings from it and the future, and possibly a need to move in a different direction. Scenarios such as the death of a spouse or parent or a traumatic divorce presents a learning experience that has now been passed through.

The identity lens is similarly constructed, often related to a role, such as being a spouse, boss, son, or outsider in a culture. This identity shift culminates in a more natural feeling or acceptance of the new way: truth seen through a different lens. Theoretically, then, the TL has led to the identity shift. This is why TL and identity are so tightly intertwined. One is the process (TL) and the other the outcome (identity), connected by the thread of reflected experiences. The new identity is no longer held hostage to the emotions of the TL, no longer motivated to focus on it and rather, settling into a new future-looking consciousness. It is like a ship sailing to a waypoint, and once passed, reveals a new compass course to the next destination in time and life.

A contemporary pressing issue in the global leadership domain is the great need for identifying, selecting, and developing those individuals who have the highest potential for this complex global leadership role. Studying global leaders and their identity development identifies and describes the role that TL plays in capacity development for global leadership roles. The findings from this work may contribute to leadership development strategies and designs for leadership learning at all levels across the lifespan and career.

This study will draw out the key dynamics that connect the three concepts of TL, identity, and global leadership development across the lifespan as viewed from the narrative, or life story.

CHAPTER THREE

———————×⋅∘◉∘⋅×———————

Research Methodology

Introduction to the Inquiry Method

This chapter builds on the literature with three interrelated goals: (a) what counted for evidence in this study, (b) what data were collected, and (c) what the data analysis process was. This study was designed to examine the relationships among transformative learning (TL), identity, leader personality, and life experiences to determine *how* and, more importantly, *when* an individual developed the capacity to lead in highly complex global organizations at the highest levels of leadership responsibility, and any other relevant factors about *when* an individual learned to lead and what he or she did with that learning and how the learning influenced his/her deontology. The study was situated primarily in TL theory with an emphasis on the transformative life experiences that affected identity and perspective transformation (also known as consciousness), the identity literature within personality psychology, and the specialized field of global leadership within the international management and leadership literatures.

This study argued for a holistic research context to examine the antecedents, critical reflections, and transformational shifts that occurred in the leaders' identities which represented an integration not only of who the person was, but also what he or she was doing in the world, and how those two things were made more congruent.

Research question. *What are the markers of successful global leaders that would account for their capacity to navigate the complexity of their roles?*

As strongly indicated by the research question, a type of narrative data counted for evidence. A survey would not have provided the necessary data nor shed significant insights. Narrative interviewing gave the fullest opportunity for participants to elaborate their stories and allowed for qualitative tools to draw out the learning experiences. This study was interested in a leader's capacity to lead, which means his or her capacity to do something specific. What he or she is doing included but goes beyond the transformative learning event(s) and a leader's identity construction to include what and how he or she was doing the leading. A narrative method was chosen to approach the phenomenon in this study— both the nature and consequences of a leader's life experiences. The narrative approach allowed an open set of insights into the less explored phenomena of identity in leadership and TL while leading by studying the private experiences of senior leaders across their lifespan. A specific type of life story approach was chosen because it guided interviewees to tell stories about eight specific scenes across their lifespan (highest point, lowest point, turning point, childhood scene, adolescent scene, adult scene). The interview also posed questions about summary points of view (habits of mind) including politics, religion, a philosophy of life, and a life theme.

The commitment to the narrative lens was particularly relevant to this study in the way it portrayed poignant life events within the context of the antecedents and futures. The narrative method, in combination with thematic analysis, provided the most objective treatment of individual data by using open coding to present the executive's story within his/her social and cultural milieu. The life stories of leaders may be best represented as a grand story line (i.e., holistically) while attempting to highlight "the often unheard of, hidden aspects of leadership resulting from their personal experience" (Turner & Mavin, 2008, p. 376). Using a life story narrative contributed to the deep biographical archive so crucial to McAdams' continuing work.

The remainder of this chapter will describe the selection design and procedures for selection.

Participant Selection Design

How Research Participants Were Recruited

For this study, it was essential to find people in global leadership positions that were challenged by their enormous responsibilities. This study sought global leaders that went through successive promotions, expatriate assignments, and challenges at the highest levels in multinational organizations across the 20th and 21st centuries—experiences that may have challenged their identity as leaders. These types of participants would be able to explain how they were challenged and what made them change in some way. If these leaders had been through something that could, by their own account, change their identity, an interview protocol would enable documentation of what they had done and will do based on these challenges. The demographic for the study goals and objectives rested on identifying the right type of general managers: Those who were working in diverse operating conditions with regular cross-cultural communications, perhaps having experienced wide swings in economic conditions, and part of a volatile, uncertain, complex, and ambiguous (VUCA) operating environment (Lemoine & James, 2014).

Sources of Participants for This Study

The participants were identified through a series of social media requests and direct contact with personal or professional relationships with executives in a referral network. Twenty prospective participants were identified through professional contacts.

Prospective participants were introduced to the study through email and provided a one and one-half page study brief. The study brief is provided in Appendix A. After an initial positive response through email, a 15-minute phone conversation was scheduled to discuss the study and the participant's responsibilities, before inviting the participant to join the study. Upon expressed interest to proceed with the study, all prospective participants received a customized Participant Administrative Letter (PAL) outlining a checklist of activities to complete for each part of the data collection. As can be seen by the PAL (see Appendix B), each participant was asked to complete the Informed Consent letter and four surveys. These surveys were designed to aid participant selection. The PAL checklist included the instructions for completing and returning the Informed Consent letter to the researcher. At this point, participants were not aware that they could be excluded from the study due to the results of these surveys.

Prospective participants were offered appointments for their 2-hour interview during the initial call, as it was difficult to schedule a lengthy appointment without sufficient planning. In the case of scheduling pressure due to the executive's limited scheduling availability, and due to the strength of the referrers for the intended participants, it seemed low risk to take the time to conduct an interview even if the participant did not later meet all the selection criteria. The only inviolate selection rule was receipt of the Informed Consent letter before the interview. Participants were likely to complete the assessments at different times due to their time availability. Participants were interviewed before they completed all the required assessments.

Participant Selection Process

The participant selection followed a detailed screening process. The selection process flow is shown in the diagram on the following page (see Figure 2).

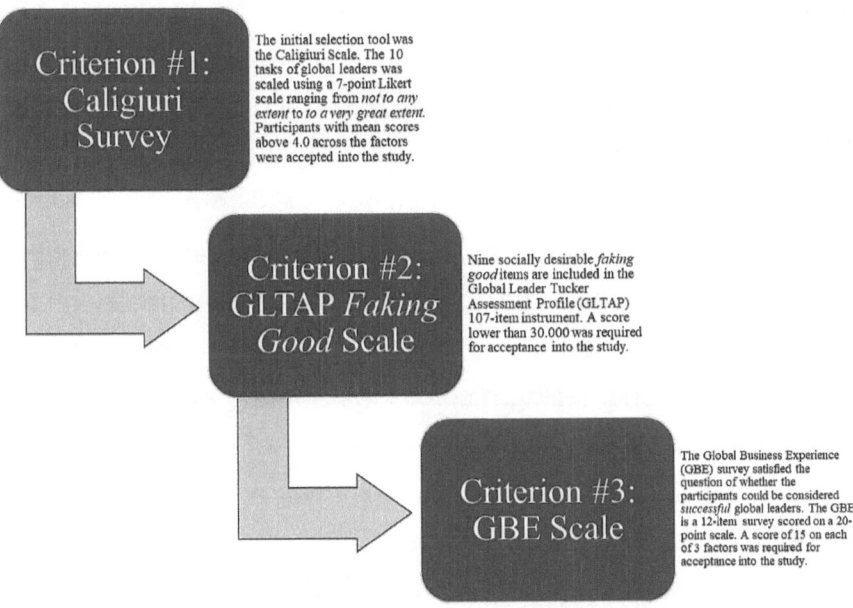

Figure 2. Participant selection criteria and process.

Three instruments were selected to aid in the final selection of participants into the study: A demographic survey, of which the Caligiuri Scale is a part, the Global Leader Tucker Assessment Profile (GLTAP), and the Global Business Experience survey (GBE).

Selection criterion #1 - Caligiuri scale. The initial selection tool was the Caligiuri scale. This scale was constructed based on the reported 10 tasks of global leaders. Caligiuri's 10 tasks of global leaders (Caligiuri, 2006, p. 220) was scaled using a 7-point Likert scale ranging from *1=not to any extent* to *7=to a very great extent.* This survey was online. On average, it took participants less than five minutes to complete this questionnaire. This scale was used for selection with the theory that transformative learning develops as leaders take on the differentiated responsibilities of leading at global scale. Some transformative learning is theorized in those areas of work, which sets the stage for subject changes in identity as a study participant assumed greater global responsibility. These responsibilities were reflected in the tasks of the global leader. Appendix F shows a mock-up of the Caligiuri questionnaire and the scale anchors for preselection.

Selection criterion #2 - the GLTAP. The second selection method was derived from the social desirability scale, or the "Faking Good" scale, of the GLTAP. To combat the arguments of participants only telling nice stories about themselves in the interviews and leaving out the shadow side of their personalities that are less conscious, the study participants completed the GLTAP instrument. The 107-item instrument included nine socially desirable, or "faking good" items (Tucker, Bonial, Vanhove, & Kedharnath, 2014, p. 6). Results of the GLTAP were analyzed and selection decisions were made before coding the interviews, to minimize time in the coding process for those participants who were deselected based on the GLTAP selection criteria. The "Social Desirability" scale was developed based on general rules that one is not "always" full of energy, usually would not say they "never" are disappointed in people, typically people would not say they are "never" bored, and so on. Extreme scores on this scale typically indicate less than honest responses, when considered as a cluster. The factor loads on a scale of 0 to 33.600. Participants with a score higher than 30.000 would be considered *fake*.

Mitigating the risk of skewed stories. The social desirability scale items appear in Appendix G. A cut score of 33.000 was used for selection.

Selection criterion #3 - Global Business Experience (GBE). The GBE scale is the third of the selection criteria. To ensure that the findings of the study were representative of high quality, successful global leaders, the study needed a method to measure success. All organizations have their own ways to measure success, which was problematic to the study. To normatively assess success factors across the participant base and to provide a satisfactory way of measuring *success*, the Global Business Experience (GBE) questionnaire was selected. The GBE is a validated psychometric instrument that measures the outcomes of success for executives in global roles. The GBE is a 12-item survey scored on a 20-point scale that reports scores for three success outcome factors: Driving Performance, Building Team Effectiveness, and Global Networking.

The cut score for inclusion into this study was a score of at least 15 on each of the three factors measured on the GBE.

Ensuring That Participants Are Exemplars

The GLTAP intercultural competencies predicted global leader success, while the GBE factors were the criteria or outcomes of global leader success. The GBE measures of success are reported in Figure 8, along with the GLTAP cultural competencies of the study participants in Figure 9.

Recruiting Results

From the pool of 20 potential participants, 16 participated in the study. Fourteen participants completed every assessment. Two participants participated in the interview but did not complete any of the assessments. The expected reasons for noncompliance of the two participants were unclear. It was expected to have been related to the executives' travel schedules, as both participants maintained a heavy international travel schedule during the research cycle.

Process to Collect Interview Data

Interviews were scheduled in advance over 3 months and conducted in person or via videoconferencing, and digitally recorded. A few interviews took place in segments over several days, due to the executive's availability. Each interview took, on average, 2 hours and 26 minutes and resulted in an average of 151 pages of transcript per interview. In total, 16 executives participated in the life story interviews.

All participants selected a four-digit code and a pseudonym as their study name to protect their anonymity. None of the participants resisted the length of the interview protocol. All participants requested a copy of their assessment results and the final report.

The interview recordings were sent electronically to the contracted transcription firm. Three typists transcribed the transcripts. The digital interview recordings have been archived electronically.

A research journal was kept for noting observations, thoughts about the participant's story, and personal reflections that the interview might have triggered. The transcriptionists also kept a journal and noted unique aspects of each interview as they were transcribing.

The life story interview data collection was, as suggested by the discussion of the McAdams interview protocol, a very detailed walk through the intimate journey of a person's life. It offered rare insights into the turning points in an individual's life—both personally and professionally. Participants described, for example, their earliest memories, their favorite stories (movies, books, or family histories), their ups and downs, and the challenges they have faced across a lifetime of significant accomplishments as a global executive in a multinational organization. This protocol offered insight into the stream of life before, during, and after life-changing transformations.

In terms of data structure, during the interview each participant was asked to identify a specific event and discuss it in detail. The participant had a personal choice about which event to talk about it. It is rather straightforward to code these events due to the protocol, although some participants told "nested" event stories (e.g., they started talking about a scene that involved one person and then added information about different people and places). The type of event was identified within each interview, which simultaneously provided an event-type code and a scene that included antecedents. Each identified theme was located in the structure of the interview which placed the event along a chronological lifeline. The age of the participant during most events was discussed in the interview as part of the McAdams' protocol, which specifically suggested such follow-up questions. When age was not asked directly by the interviewer, the participant generally offered the age at the time of the event without prompting.

The transcripts from the interviews that were created from the interview protocol represented an initial hard coding schema albeit insensitive to the research question. There were more than 2,500 pages of transcripts available for coding. Transcripts were analyzed using the coding feature in Dedoose according to the open coding method, as planned. As contemplated by the plan outlined in the Method discussion, five participant transcripts were coded in three cycles to establish a codebook. The codebook became the analytical tool for coding the remaining 11 interviews. An explanation of the coding cycles will provide insight into the results of this narrative interview research.

Data Collection Procedures

The Life Story Interview

This study relied on a protocol that ensured the storyline of each participant was complete, or as complete as possible due to autobiographical convenience of self-awareness of the participant. The life history data collection of this study used the nine-category McAdams interview protocol (www.sesp. northwestern.edu/docs/Interviewrevised95.pdf); (McAdams, 1995). The nine topics included in the interview are noted in Appendix H.

The interview was conducted in person or via web-enabled videoconferencing and was recorded. All participants selected a four-digit code and created a pseudonym as their study name to protect their anonymity. Each interview was scheduled for 90 minutes in length, with 30 minutes on either end of the interview to allow for setting up the recording equipment and settling into the interview, as well as anticipating the need for additional time, based primarily on a pilot study experience.

The online interview recording was saved electronically in two forms: (a) The software resident in the video-teleconferencing system, and (b) A thumb drive that recorded audio. In the case of recording an in-person interview, two forms of recording devices were used: A thumb drive connected to a laptop; dialing into the recorded videoconferencing system. The interviews were transcribed by a third-party service which signed a non-disclosure agreement which has been kept on file with the research archives. All digital recordings were deleted by the typing service. The printed transcripts and the digital interview files are on a 5-year archive schedule.

Narrative Interview Coding Procedures

The commitment of the narrative lens on a lifespan was particularly helpful to this study, as it was essential to see the poignant life events within the context of the antecedents and futures. Despite the lack of an organizing principle for the interview, many options existed for coding and comparing the global narratives across research communities. McAdams does not report a specific method for coding his life story interviews. As to the manner of coding this study data, it was compelling to use Lieblich's Holistic-Content Perspective (Lieblich, Tuval-Mashiach, & Zilber, 1998), Bohn and Berntsen's 42 Life Script Events (Bohn & Berntsen, 2008), Habermas and Bluck's (2000) four types of coherence (i.e., temporal, biographical, causal, and thematic), or Hoggan's (2016) 28 distinct codes and six broad categories of the TL metanalytical outcomes represented by the stories. However, in keeping with the descriptive nature of the research, and ensuring reliability and validity to this naturalistic study, open thematic coding was chosen as the preferred method.

Interview Coding Results

The results of the interview were raw transcript data. The transcripts were imported into Dedoose and initially organized within the nine categories of the interview protocol. The interview data were analyzed electronically through thematic coding under each of the nine interview categories in the life story. The data were exported from Dedoose into Microsoft Excel for further statistical analysis by the codebook.

The first coding cycle. Three interviews were selected at random based on the availability of transcripts. Two researchers, the primary researcher and a second coder, used the Dedoose software to organize the data and conduct an open coding analysis on three interviews. Multiple themes emerged within each of the interview categories. The most frequently mentioned, most common answers to each question category were arranged as codes in descending order in a table reporting the findings. Two researchers coded the first three transcripts without a code book to develop the codes independently. The first research team meeting focused on the codes generated for those interviews. Twenty-two codes were reviewed in detail and modified.

The second coding cycle. A second coding was conducted with a revised list of codes by both researchers, and two additional interviews were added, thus making this an analysis of five participants. This coding cycle resulted in 20 codes. Disagreements in coding were discussed at a meeting, along with observations about the overall life story themes that were emerging. The research team independently coded and recoded the same five transcripts after each codebook change.

The third coding cycle. Both researchers completed three cycles of analysis of the first five interviews. In the end, the fundamental differences in the final codebook reflected five additional unique codes by the primary researcher and 19 codes related to the McAdams categories, resulting in 36 open codes. Final disagreements were resolved over email. The level of agreement on the 36 open codes was 86.1%. The primary researcher completed coding the remaining interviews with the established codebook. The official codebook is provided in Appendix C.

All categories were cross-checked by the pair of researchers and they agreed upon the final coding. It was anticipated that once a theme (coding category) had been established through at least three interviews, one or two additional interviews would be coded until that theme had been saturated. Once saturation was achieved, the open coding stopped. At that point, the study codes (the *codebook*) were deemed established. From that point on, the primary researcher completed coding the remaining interviews with the fixed codebook.

A method to identify and then parse the life story into those experiences that were transformative and nontransformative was designed using the Mezirow definition of meaning making. These data are presented in a table. Those data that represented TL were further separated into identity and non-identity events units. The Illeris definition of identity was used for this sorting procedure. Finally, a table representing the actual raw coding based on the nine categories of the McAdams interview was required to discern a pattern amongst the participants at different stages of their lives. This study was able to describe in detail the nature and description of those events through the eyes of the person who experienced them. Therefore, there were three additional tables of data to compare (a) experiences themed as "transformative" or "nontransformative," (b) events that represent "identity-development" and "nonidentity development" transformative learning, and (c) the ages at which both data (1) and data (2) were reported. Additional tables were created identifying the antecedents of TL, which listed the types of event triggers occurring for TL, the type(s) of situations that were expected (e.g., cultural, familial) versus unexpected (e.g., job loss), and a comparison of the experiences with the character of the global leader.

Narrative Interview Analysis

The second level of analysis in the interviews was global coherence, which was a high-level view across all interviews, depicting a "grand story" that stood out. An emerging grand storyline was made note of and considered as a potential new point of analysis for the coding. That analysis began with the question: *What stood out from the open coding?* The next step was sorting the data by demographics: Gender, country of birth, country of education, spousal country of origin, host country, and so forth. Tables were prepared reporting the demographics of the study sample.

Following a thorough review of all data, categories, and coherence to a grand storyline, analysis was focused on isolating that data which answered the research question most directly. Toward that end, answers to three questions were summarized:

1. Descriptions of transformative learning and identity change, comparing the terminology used for both and ways to determine if they were, in fact, the same thing.
2. A way to capture whether the narrative of life experiences documented the centrality of narrative to ongoing identity formation in any way.
3. The age at which the eight critical life events occurred (McAdams' question number 2).

The psychometric data (e.g., the GLTAP) provided a method of analysis for coding the extent of the executive's worldview, personality, and social/interpersonal style. The GBE provided additional success criteria with which to gauge other useful insights from the interview data.

Summary of Research Methodology

In conclusion, this chapter described the research methodology for a qualitative study that uncovered the antecedents of transformative life experiences, a description of those life experiences, and the reflections on the meaning made from those experiences as a global leader evolved his/her life and career. This chapter has identified what counted for evidence in answering the research question, how participants were selected and data gathered to answer that question, how each participant was interviewed thoroughly according to the McAdams interview protocol to discern their life story, and then the examination of the text of those resulting transcripts according to a structured analytical plan. This plan leaves open that this study collected data that McAdams would not have anticipated. Chapter 4 describes what happened when we followed this plan.

CHAPTER FOUR

Report of Data
and Study Findings

This chapter is organized as a descriptive report of the evidence (interview findings), especially those related to the research question. The research plan was carried out according to the planned research design. An explanation of what accounted for response patterns, particularly those of primary importance to the research question, is presented. A discussion follows of any ambiguity in the data or identifying questions left unanswered. Finally, the findings are presented in tables and figures. The remainder of this chapter describes the collected data, how it was analyzed, and a discussion of the findings from the analysis as it begins to answer the research question by showing the relationships between the data. In addition, a space was kept for the data that came from the prescreening process that provided additional data for analysis.

Selection Results

The Caligiuri Selection Report

The Caligiuri survey was completed by 14 of the 16 participants. This survey and the data from the questionnaire are reported as *The Caligiuri Scale*. Participant 1961, "Bonnie," was excluded from the study due to the Caligiuri Scale. This participant had a mean score of 2.8, indicating that this current participant's responsibilities were insufficiently global. The participant's scores were affected by six factors: Language skills and responsibilities for global strategy, budget, negotiation, suppliers/vendors, and risk management. Participant 1961's interview data were removed from analysis and are not reported in the study findings, although her assessment data will be reported in some figures for reference. It should be noted, however, that Participant 1961 had high scores in the other pre-selection criteria. It is possible that Participant 1961 is a highly competent global leader but is not in a sufficiently global role to leverage all of her well-developed skillsets.

GLTAP Selection Results

As reported by the GLTAP administrator, Participant "Dave" triggered the *Social Desirability Scale* by 0.2222. After a careful examination of *Dave's* other data, and discussion with the instrument's publisher, it was determined that *Dave* should not be excluded from the study. The rationale for keeping *Dave* in the study is that the data from the ALP, GBE, and life story interview indicated that it was likely that *Dave* responded in a truthful way, providing good, honest responses to the interview questions.

GBE Selection Results

All participants scored above the 15.0 cut score measurement, meaning that all participants satisfied this inclusion criteria. Therefore, the study validates that each participant selected into the study was a successful global leader.

Summary of the Selection Process

The selection process was successful in admitting only high quality, successful leaders into the study. The participants are primarily North American and Northern European and were predominantly male. There were four women leaders in the participant pool. All leaders work for multinational organizations and have broad global responsibilities for managing employees, clients, and vendors globally.

This study pivots on the selection of participants who are experienced, successful global leaders. As discussed in the Methodology, great care was made to select participants based on three specific criteria. Further to the results of these selection criteria, Figure 3 shows the extent to which these global leaders exceed the Caligiuri Scale (where 1=*low*, and 7=*high*) on the 10 tasks of global leadership. Only one participant failed to meet the criteria. With the selection process successfully completed, the collection of the interview data will be discussed.

Additional tables and figures follow, reporting descriptive statistics including data about the characteristics of participants, including matrices of participant demographics. What the participants said, and the multiple levels of significance of their stories, are shown across the remainder of this chapter.

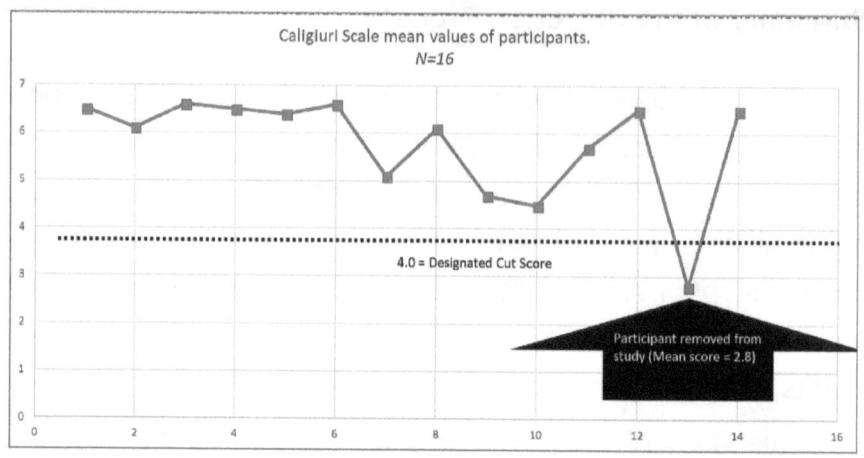

X axis = Number of participants
Y axis = Mean Caligiuri Scale values

Figure 3. Caligiuri[7] Scale mean values of participants.

Figure 3 shows the computed mean values of the Caligiuri Survey responses for 14 of the 16 participants. Fourteen participants were selected for the study, as they scored at least a 4.0 mean score on the Caligiuri Scale. The 4.0 mean cut score represents the participant's task-related work experience at global scale, which was rated *to an extent*, which is the least amount of global responsibility acceptable in this study.

Special Considerations for Selection

Many of the participants' lowest scoring item on the Caligiuri Scale was Item #21, *I may need to speak in a language other than my mother tongue at work.* Forty-six percent (46%) of the study participants were below a mean score of 4 on language;

---

[7] Reprinted from Human Resource Management Review, 16, Paula Caligiuri, Developing global leaders, 219-228., Copyright (2006), with permission from Elsevier. License #4366210389191,

however, even with this variable being a low score, it was not the specific cause of any participant's removal from the study. It would be useful to determine the significance of this variable. This issue is addressed in Chapter 6 as a potential future study interest. For purposes of this study, only one global leader ("John") reported taking time to specifically learn another language to improve the chances of obtaining an international assignment. As noted in his interview, language was important criteria for a position in Mexico for his company, and at the time of his first application for an expatriate assignment, he spoke no Spanish. This is how *John* reported his language abilities:

I networked my way to meet somebody down there and she basically said, "You're a nice person and all, but you're about as far from the skill set of what we need . . . like you're selling [redacted] to governments in Kentucky and we are a [redacted] network to governments in Kentucky. We are a [redacted] company selling to the, you know, consumer segment in South America in Spanish." She was like, "You're like a, 'Does Not Qualify.'" Don't even enter, kind of, was the feedback. So, I said, well okay. I got that. So, I started taking Spanish classes and paying for them out of my own pocket and, you know, started trying. . . (John)

Demographics of the Selected Participant Group

Demographics were collected in two ways: (a) a survey that included the Caligiuri questions, and (b) the GLTAP demographic questions. Table 4 reports the participant demographics from the online survey, which includes factors which may prove helpful in future research. Variables relevant to this study are age, gender, and citizenship. There were five Americans, two each from France, Germany, the Netherlands, and the United Kingdom. One participant each was Canadian, Lebanese, and Ukrainian. Note that one German participant reported Austria as his birth country and reported citizenship as German.

The second set of demographic data from the GLTAP reported additional occupational details including industry, job title, and time in position. These additional data will be useful in future analysis.

Table 4

Online Demographic Survey collected through Survey Monkey

Participant Code	Nationality (Father)	Nationality (Mother)	# of Siblings	Birth Order	Country Origin	Year of Birth	Age	Citizenship (Self)	Citizenship (Spouse)	Current Host Country	# of Children	Educational Country			Gender
												Primary	College	Master's	
3132	US	US	2	Eldest	US	1954	63	US	US	US	0	US	US	US	Male
2355	UK	UK	3	Second	UK	1959	58	UK	UK	UK	0	UK	UK	UK	Male
1234	FR	FR	2	Youngest	FR	1960	57	FR	ES-CH	ES	4	FR	FR	FR	Male
3033	US	US	3	Youngest	US	1960	57	US	-	US	1	US	US	US	Male
1952	US	US	5	Adopted	LB	1952	53	US	US	US	-	US	US	-	Male
0406	NL	NL	1	Second	NL	1964	53	NL	NL	US	1	NL	NL	US	Male
0594	DE	DE	1	Eldest	AT	1965	52	DE	US	US	2	US	US	US	Male
2711	NL	NL	0	Only	NL	1967	50	NL	NL	UK	3	NL	NL	NL	Male
0909	FR	FR	1	Eldest	FR	1967	50	FR	FR	FR	3	FR	FR	FR	Male
4067	US	US	2	Eldest	US	1967	50	US	US	CO	3	US	US	US	Male
4324	DE	US	5	Fourth	US	1968	49	US	US	US	2	US	US	US	Male
2146	US	US	0	Only	US	1970	47	US	UK	UK	0	US	US	US	Male
2210	UK	UK	1	Youngest	UK	1970	47	UK	UK	UK	2	UK	UK	UK	Male
2508	UA	UA	1	Eldest	UA	1975	42	UA	US	UA	3	UA	UA	US	Female
1961	CA	CA	2	Eldest	CA			CA		US	1	-	-	-	Female
3282	DATA NOT PROVIDED														Female

COUNTRY	COUNTRY CODE
Switzerland	CH
Germany	DE
Netherlands, The	NL
Ukraine	UA

COUNTRY	COUNTRY CODE
France	FR
Austria	AT
United Kingdom	UK
United States	US

COUNTRY	COUNTRY CODE
Colombia	CO
Canada	CA
Spain	ES
Lebanon	LB

Table 5

GLTAP Demographics

Participant Code	Industry	Job Title	Nationality	Current Country of Residence	Current City of Residence	Time in Current Position-Yr.
1961	Transportation/ Trucking/Railroad	EVP & Chief Practice Officer	Canada	United States of America	Monrovia, MD	1
3033	Airlines/Aviation	Sr. VP Worldwide Sales	United States of America	United States of America	Chicago	13
0594	Information Technology and Services	Sr. Vice President	Germany	United States of America	Boston	2
4324	Architecture & Planning	President and CEO	United States of America	United States of America	Panama City Beach, FL	5
3132	Market Research	Chairman	United States of America	United States of America	Austin	33
2210	Consumer Goods	President, Europe	United Kingdom	United Kingdom	Reigate	3
2146	Oil & Energy	Chief Talent Officer	United States of America	United Kingdom	London	5
0909	Consumer Goods	Managing Director European Food Service	France	France	Rueil Malmaison	2
1234	Consulting	Partner	France	Spain	Barcelona	2
2508	Non-Profit Organization Management	IFES Eurasia Director of Training	Ukraine	Ukraine	Kyiv	5
2711	Food & Beverages	Managing Director	Netherlands	United Kingdom	Woking	1
2355	Consumer Goods	EVP	United Kingdom	Denmark	Copenhagen	1
0406	Power Generation	Top Business Executive (President)	Netherlands	United States of America	Charlotte	3
4067	Internet telecommunications	Country Manager	United States	Columbia	Bogata	Not provided

Note. 1952 and 3282 did not complete the GLTAP.

Interview Findings

Most participants commented that the interview format provided them a "unique opportunity to reflect" and remember "almost lost memories." At the end of each interview, participants expressed gratitude for the opportunity of being able to take the time to go through this process and expressed that it left them reflective at the end of the interview. The study participants reflected on several important outcomes of their life: reflection on the most meaningful value in human living, projection of a good future (or their worst fears for a negative future), and what they thought would best describe their philosophy of life. They narrated a description of their political and religious views, and how those views had changed over time.

For descriptive purposes, the 1,472 events were classified into the final codebook categories. This resulted in 47 categories. The top seven categories by count weight included five McAdams interview protocol questions. The 47 coded experiences cluster into several meta themes. While there are many exciting data, the next level of analysis now turns to the research question to isolate those data that would serve to answer the research question. The analysis of those data is organized by meta themes which mirrors the GLTAP framework in Table 6.

Just 14 of the life experience categories account for 61% of the total 1,472 events described in the interviews. Twenty-four of the coded life experience categories account for 80% of the total events. The top five types of reported life experiences relate directly to the research question and represent 54.6% of the top 14 event categories, and 32% of the total. The data most directly applicable to the research question are the codes presented in Table 6.

Some types of life experiences reported appeared to be related to the capacity to lead complex global organizations. These transcripts were analyzed to identify which events were transformational (life changing) and how those events were set into the life context to illuminate the antecedents. Relevant interview excerpts are organized in context for the top five coded life experience categories. In these excerpts the text is treated to portray the differences between triggers and transformational impacts. This treatment is especially useful in the Turning Points data. These data are contained in Table 7.

Table 6

Meta Themes from the Coded Experiences

Descriptor	Theme	Experience Type
Distal	Values Beliefs Personality Characteristics Philosophy of Life	Experiences that challenged value systems, personal philosophy, beliefs, exhibited personality characteristics in action (behaviors), the deontological framework of the leader
Proximal	Competencies Developed	Experiences that developed competencies for global leadership
Leadership Criteria	Business Environment Processes Success Area (specialty) Leader Advancement Model	Experiences related to: • Effects of the economic collapse of 2008; business failure • Promotions; demotions; termination • Sales success; Industry specific skill success • Effects of succession planning

Table 7

Top Five Categories of Coded Life Experiences by Weighting of 1,472 Events

Code	Number of Reported Experiences	Sample Descriptors (Most frequently mentioned types of experiences)
Transformational Turning Points	130	• Job changes in mid-career after 20+ years on the job • Leaving a new company after only 2 years due to values issues • Big promotions • Several promotions followed by an embarrassing failure • "The Moses Factor" (participants referenced business failures and their way to serenely persevere in the face of failure)[3] • Marriage • Divorce • Death of spouse • Death of parent • First child born • Significant health problem
Values	107	• Sense of duty and responsibility; teaching children the importance of responsibility • Independent thinking • Helping/supporting others • Importance of family • Self-awareness • Making the world a better place • High morality even if it made them less popular (no smoking, heavy drinking, etc.) • Open, honest, transparent communication • Servant leadership
Work Ethic	95	• Outworked everyone else • Plain, old hard work • Fear of failure • Not feeling adequately qualified for the next big job • Followed the "American Dream"

Influencers	87	• Father
		• Best friend's father
		• Mother
		• Boss/mentor
		• Community business leader
Stories watched, read, or heard	69	• The Brothers Karamazov
		• Hans Solo (Star Wars)
		• Rudy (The movie)
		• Grandfather

Note. Most stories have a moral directly related to their own life experiences

In summary, the life story interviews were clear and compelling both in terms of triggers, struggles, and transformations that each participant experienced. It was fascinating to hear how emotionally and mentally strong each participant was, and how important it was for each of them to follow their own path which frequently put them on a trajectory quite different from their families of origin and in some cases, their closest friends. In addition, the expressed values the participants live by are clear, as are examples of their work ethic, the significance of the influencers on their lives, and how stories that are meaningful to them related back to their lives. While many people facing these challenges might find the barriers to success insurmountable, these participants showed the grit and perseverance to meet the challenge each time – whether that challenge was the death of a loved one, or getting fired, or not getting the job desired. In other words, the magnitude of the challenge and the type of challenge presented seemed unimportant to the individual.

Other Findings

The interview data were robust, and as a result, five more analyses were conducted than proposed in the Methodology chapter. It is important to understand other findings because they have the potential to address additional nuances of the research question. In total, 11 additional analyses were conducted on the interviews, as follows:

1. A listing of all representative events along a chronological life line (X-axis) and a general measure of the importance or severity of the transformation along the Y-axis. The importance or severity of the experience was ranked Low (L), Medium (M), or High (H) based on the interview notes. The analysis is shown by Figure 4.

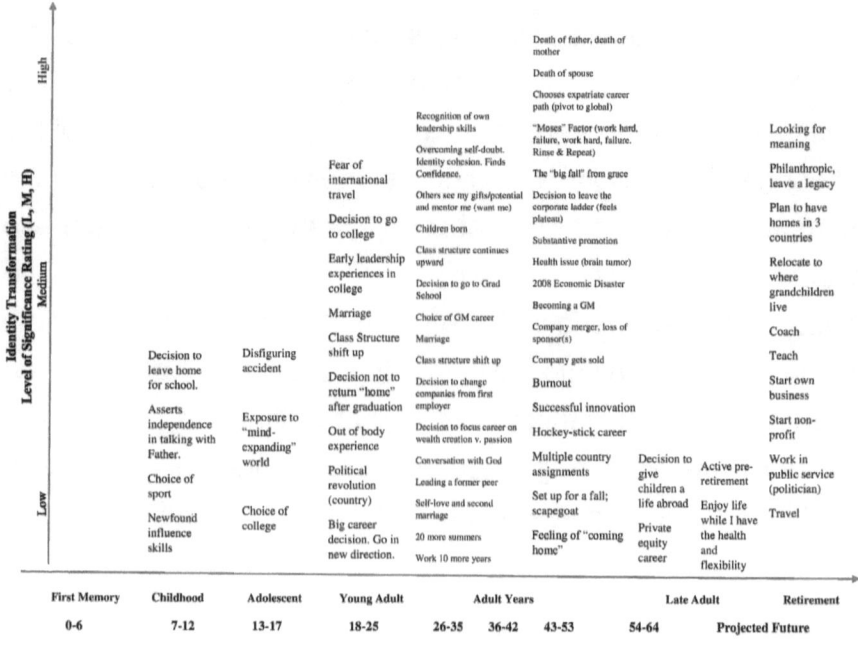

Figure 4. Levels of severity of transformative events across the lifespan.

Locating experiences which were transformative (Type 1, provoking a change in direction or Type 2, not provoking a change in direction) are shown in Table 8. The other axes are coded Type 3 (identity changing experience), or Type 4 (non-identity changing experience). There was no need to force fit a definition of identity change with transformation because the participant gave a clear, verbal signal of the type of experience and how it affected his/her identity and the life trajectory. The four types are combined in a 2 x 2 matrix in Table 8.

Table 8

Matrix of Transformative and Identity-Changing Experiences

Transformative Experiences	**Nontransformative (Less Transformative) Experiences**
TYPE 1 • Some experiences before age 7 (i.e., traumatic wound care in orphanage at age 3) • Peak life experience • Nadir (lowest) life experience • Turning Point • Significant Promotions • Expatriation • Important Scenes (child, adolescence, adult, one additional experience from any era) • Business failures; getting "sidelined" in one's career • Projected Futures	**TYPE 2** • Most experiences before age 7 • Most job experiences

Identity-Developmental Experiences		Non-Identity-Developmental Experiences
TYPE 3		**TYPE 4**
• Some experiences before age 7 • (i.e., gardening with father; laying on the hood of a blue car looking up at the tree limbs projecting next summer being able to climb the tree with the older kids) • Getting fired • Mentor and significant influencer interactions • Projected futures with health; fears of negative marital arrangements after retirement		• Not found in the interviews

2. A chronological timeline (the X-axis) across the lifespan with age as the Y-axis showing all participant experiences. This is summarized in Figure 5.

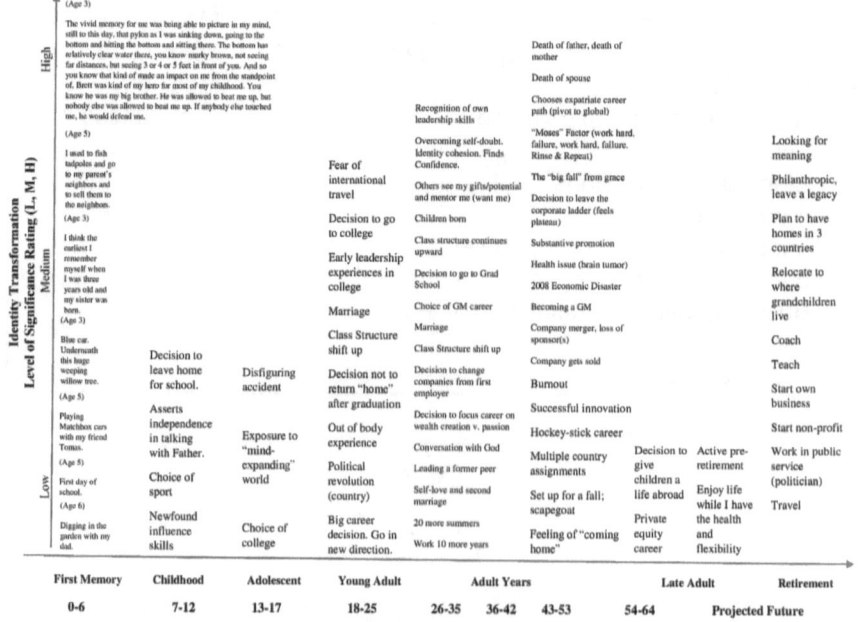

Figure 5. *Identity transformation by reported age.*

3.   Figure 6 provides an overlay of the participants' four-digit codes and self-actualization scores. This provides a visualization of those with higher self-actualization scores (from the ALP) along with the experiences. Additional research is recommended to determine the significance of early, memorable and significant life experiences that related to developing capacity and the self-actualization score. Of particular interest is "Berg," who described a terrorizing near-drowning experience at age 3.

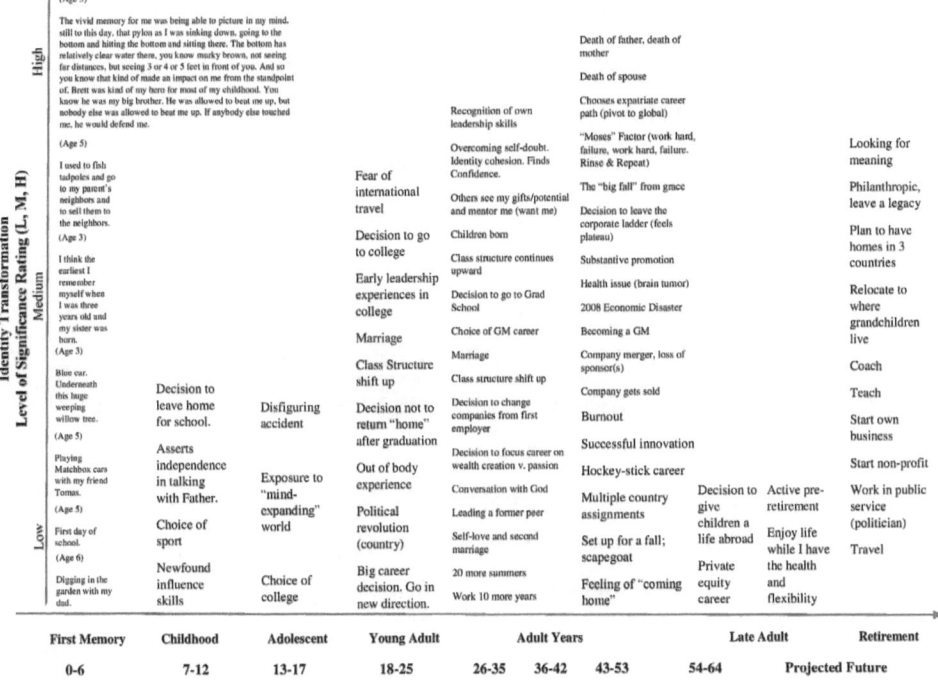

Figure 6.   Transformations reported by participants.
(Note: Self-actualization scores are contained in parenthesis)

4. Table 9 is an interpretive table for Figure 7, further refining the X and Y axes, which are represented for one exemplar participant. An analysis that traces the experiences that motivated the change, compared to Kegan's five-stage mental complexity model (see Chapter 2, Literature Review). This analysis shows the conscious realization and fulfillment of "being-ness" or identity across the lifespan in specific time horizons (shown by the X axis). For purposes of this analysis, the time horizons are shown as t1, t2, t3, t4, and t5, as the exact age of the transformative experience is less important to the analysis than the path of the experience.

    The results shown in Table 9 showed when the participant had a realization of his identity shifts. Kegan's model of consciousness development provides a way to capture the storyline and represent the subject's evolving conscious awareness of "becoming." This participant was chosen for his clear storyline and high self-actualization score. This chart shows the increasing interest in complexity, and the transcript from the interview describes how "John" made meaning from the complexity at each level cited. This analysis suggests that there is a conscious realization and fulfillment of one's being-ness, or identity as increasingly complex circumstances are attempted.

Table 9

Tracing Experiences that Motivated TL and Identity Change

Kegan Consciousness Level (Evolving Consciousness of Becoming)	Types of Reported Experiences
5 – Self-Transforming	Philosophical Reflections
4 – Self-Authoring	The Big Failure
3 - Socializing	Three to Four Promotions
2 - Instrumental	Expatriation/Resettlement
1 - Impulsive	Exposure to New Socioeconomic Experiences
0 – Not Modeled	Provincial Path (staying in the small town where "Pierre" was born and making little change)

This analysis showed when the participant had a realization of his identity shifts. Kegan's model of consciousness development provides a way to capture the storyline and represent the subject's evolving conscious awareness of "becoming." John was chosen for his clear storyline and high self-actualization score. This chart shows the increasing interest in complexity, and the transcript from the interview describes how John made meaning from the complexity at each level cited. This analysis suggests that there is a conscious realization and fulfillment of one's being-ness, or identity as increasingly complex circumstances are attempted.

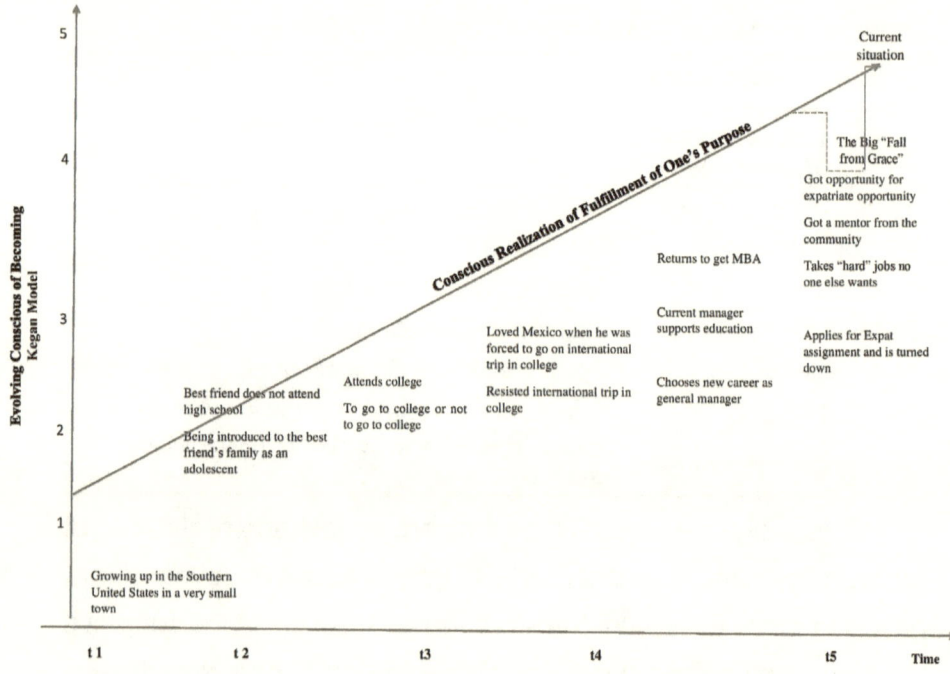

Figure 7. Tracing experiences that motivate TL and identity change (John). *Note.* Read the diagram from the bottom up in each time horizon

5.   The transformative learning phases were clearly delineated by several examples in each life story interview. One specific episode of all 10 phases of the Mezirow TL process was described by "Berg" during college, as he left the scene of a "night on the town" by a group of male friends. The participant broke away from the group based on a moral issue (the group was heading from bar to bar and finally, to a strip club). On the way back to campus, Berg and another friend stopped at a Catholic school. The school had a weekend festival with electric rides. The two sober boys enjoyed riding on the

closed festival rides for a while, and then broke into a building so Berg could play the piano. They were caught by the campus police and brought up on charges of breaking and entering. This disorienting dilemma faced by Berg took him through each of the 10 phases of Mezirow's model, resolving himself to understand the consequences of his actions; that is, "a reintegration into one's life on the basis of conditions dictated by one's new perspective" (Mezirow & Associates, 1991). This interview excerpt is so graphic, that an example may be helpful:

> The detachment commander needs to be notified. What is worse yet is the cadet commandant of students had to be notified. Major [redacted]. So, we had to go in and tell her what we had done. Now I'm faced with . . . I'm here on scholarship, and there is no way I can pay for this not being on military scholarship. It was a 4-year scholarship that I earned through academic excellence in high school—a very competitive scholarship. And if I don't have this, I'm out. And, by the way, if I don't complete the degree that the military is sending me there for the previous three years, I am required to enlist in the military as an enlisted person. (Berg)

6. The second level of analysis of the "Grand Storyline" is global coherence which is a high-level view across all interviews depicting a "grand story" that stands out. One way to capture the narrative of life experience and its centrality to the ongoing phenomenon of identity formation is represented by Figure 7. Most of the participants had a similar track, even down to the "big failure" after years

of continuous promotions and significant increases in financial rewards. Figure 7 also provides the global coherence across the entire interview group based on the life story protocol, from early childhood through to the projected futures anticipated by the participants.

7. What stands out from the open coding? It is useful to note that the open coding provided for a robust analysis within the pre-defined life story interview categories. This storyline began as a chronology but was not restrictive to chronology as the interview evolved. Many participants jumped from adult experiences to adolescent experiences throughout the interview. It seems clear that the early life experiences the individuals received (the nurturing) played heavily into their values development. The personality development is also quite clear throughout the interview, with most participants becoming morally clear and definite about their future path, on average, by the age of 17. Whether this is unique to global leaders and a defining variable, or the antecedent to their career success, or is typical of the general population cannot be verified by this study.

8. Descriptions of transformative learning and identity change, comparing the terminology used for both.

9. Events were described by the participant as triggers for change that led to life-turning points. A selection of the triggers is provided below:

    a. Promotion to Chief Operating Officer after years of climbing the ladder

    b. Being nominated as class representative in junior year of high school

c. Promoted to third baseman (realization that he was "actually one of the better people on the A Team")

d. Career decision at age 20

e. Significant health problem (brain tumor) that led to reidentifying life's purpose

f. Becoming part of the "in" crowd in college

g. Fear of international travel led to desire to become an expatriate

h. Crowning achievement in career led to a "Big Fall" from grace

i. Doing a job that you love that feeds your soul, or getting out (participant got out)

10. Event triggers that occurred just before or simultaneously with the transformations described as Turning Points. These are the antecedents to the experience. These data are embedded in the transcripts, with a selection provided for context here:

- On being promoted to third baseman:

  "Wow, really? Because I'm actually not that good at baseball, and why am I on the A team, and why are you putting me at third base to go play infield?"

Jim described his experience up to that point being a kid that "didn't assimilate." Since baseball is the quintessential American game, and he grew up in another country and his classmates grew up playing since they could walk, Jim was shocked by being good enough to be put on the A team. He describes the realization that he really was good and that he did fit in (the transformative learning experience that changed his identity):

> When this kid hit a line drive right at third base, right where I was standing, and I reached out and I caught this ball. And I remember just being like, "I caught that ball! I got it!" And everybody came up to me and was like, "Yeah, nice catch. That was great play." But to me, it was like this symbol of, "You know what? I sort of, kind of, belong!" I remember that moment and the feeling of that moment, and that was a powerful moment, actually. (Jim)

As can be seen across the life story analysis, the terminology of transformation, transformative learning experiences, or identity change–by whatever term preferred by scholars–is descriptive of the same types of experiences in this study. As the literature suggests, the terminology is not a meaningful matter.

Reported Findings from the Psychometric Assessments

The three psychometric instruments were completed by each of the study participants: The GBE, which reports the outcome measures of success in global roles; the GLTAP, which measures the specific competencies required of successful global leaders; and the ALP, which describes the self-actualization score, the shadow personality type, and the motivators of behavior for a leader.

Global Business Experience (GBE) Analysis

The GBE was administered to compare the extent of this cohort's experience compared to the Tucker database from nine nationalities of 698 leaders. In so doing, the GBE validates that each participant was a "global leader," within the GBE construct. Figure 8 shows the relationship of the three factors that significantly predict success for global leaders for the sample set. The three factors are "Driving Performance," "Building Team Effectiveness," and "Global Networking." The cut score for entry into this study was a 15.0 on each measure. As can be seen by Figure 8, all participants scored within or above the mean in the three factors of outcomes for success as a global leader. The chart provides the participants' individual scores.

The value of the GBE is creating a standardized measure of success across a global participant pool from different industries. The GBE measures potential success and is a substitute variable for other individualized measures such as performance measures within the company which are difficult to validate.

Figure 8. Profile for success in global leadership as measured by GBE.

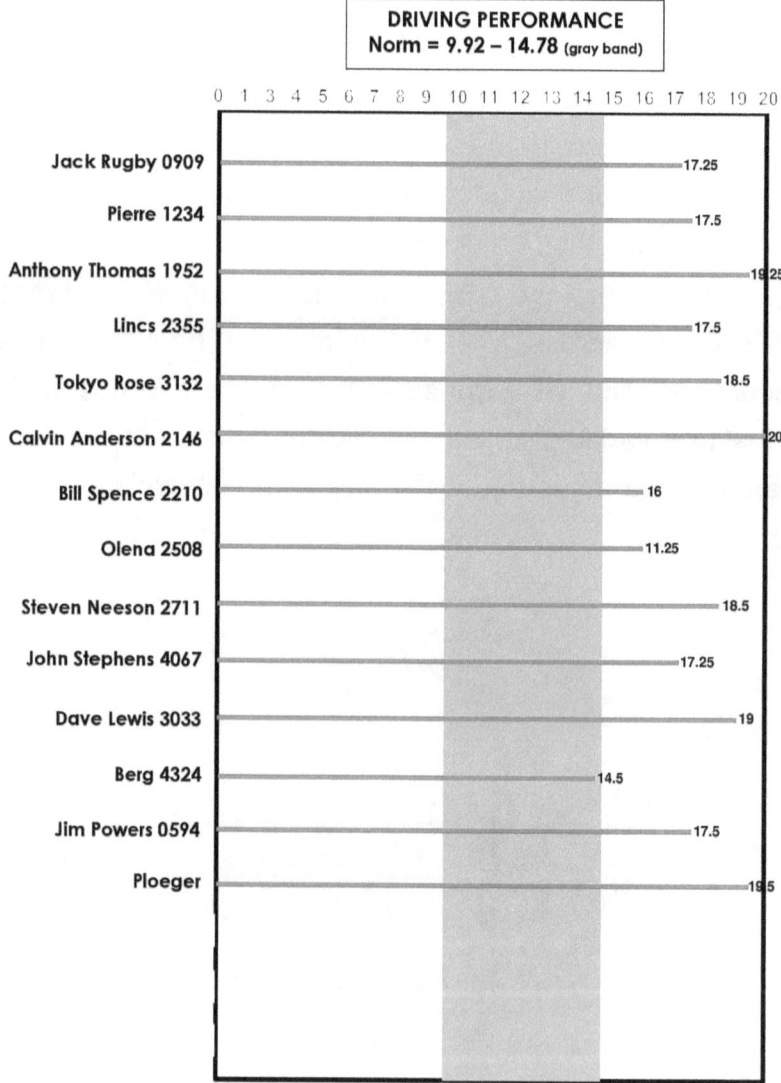

GBE (Survey of Global Business Experience)

Database = 698 Leaders of 9 Nationalities

DRIVING PERFORMANCE
Norm = 9.92 – 14.78 (gray band)

0 1 3 4 5 6 7 8 9 10 11 12 13 14 15 16 17 18 19 20

Jack Rugby 0909	17.25
Pierre 1234	17.5
Anthony Thomas 1952	19.25
Lincs 2355	17.5
Tokyo Rose 3132	18.5
Calvin Anderson 2146	20
Bill Spence 2210	16
Olena 2508	11.25
Steven Neeson 2711	18.5
John Stephens 4067	17.25
Dave Lewis 3033	19
Berg 4324	14.5
Jim Powers 0594	17.5
Ploeger	19.5

Figure 9. GBE: Driving Performance Results for this cohort.

GBE (Survey of Global Business Experience)

Database = 698 Leaders of 9 Nationalities

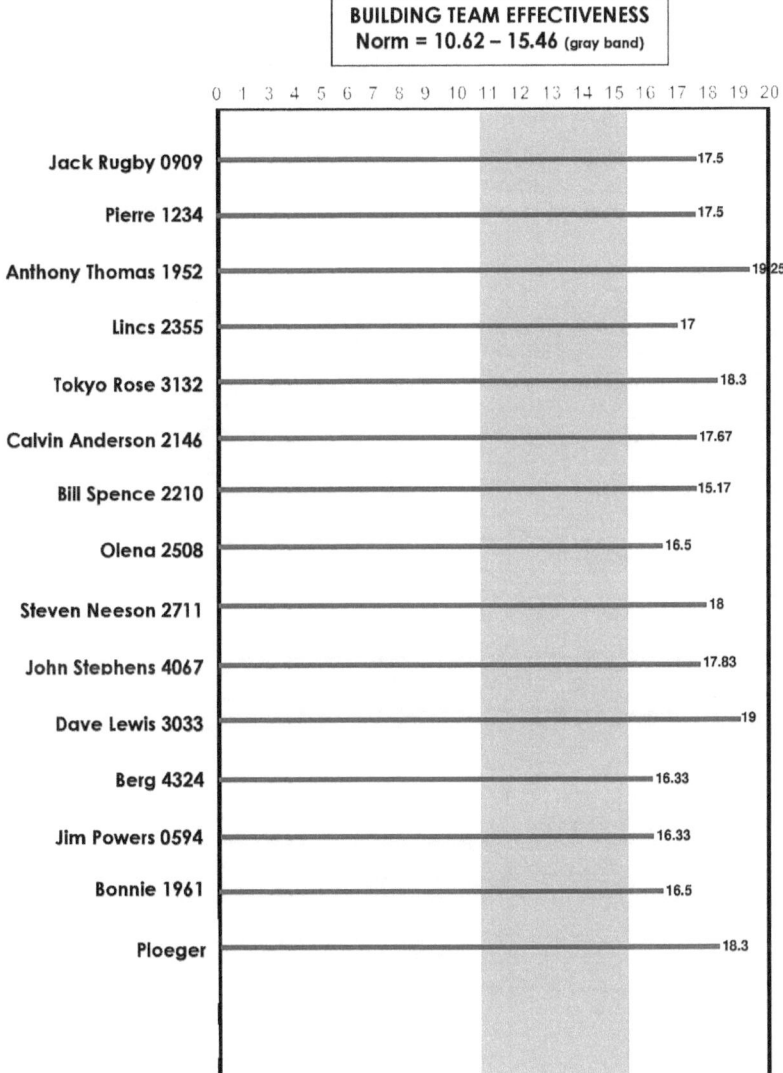

Figure 10. GBE: Building Team Effectiveness results for this cohort.

GBE (Survey of Global Business Experience)

Database = 698 Leaders of 9 Nationalities

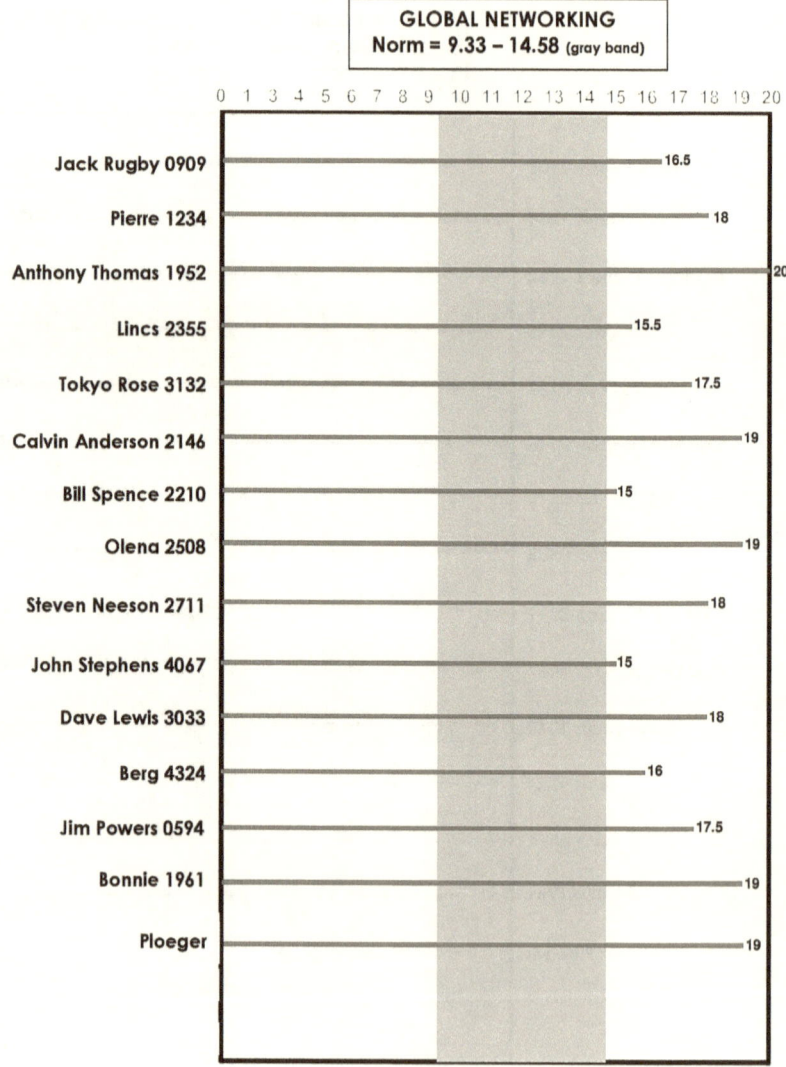

Figure 11. GBE: Global Networking results for this cohort.

Global Leader Tucker Assessment Profile (GLTAP) Analysis

The second psychometric in this study for selection is the GLTAP. The mean of the group shows that, compared to the database of 1,880 global leaders, this group profiles as highly competent as measured on the nine competency dimensions of the GLTAP. The cohort reports above the norms on five competencies of global leadership, which become *markers*:

1. Open-Mindedness
2. Locus of Control
3. Demonstrating Creativity
4. Adapting Socially
5. Instilling Trust

The cohort reports in the norms on four global competencies:

1. Lifetime Learning
2. Patience
3. Even Disposition
4. Instilling Trust

The following charts show several useful analyses of the GLTAP data as compared to the instrument's norm. Figure 12 shows the highest reported competencies, Figure 13 shows the lowest reported competencies, Figure 14 shows a scattergram of the sample, and Figure 15 shows the over/under one standard deviation from the mean, and Figure 16 shows the net difference scores between this sample and the norm group. As can be seen by these charts, this group is not only highly competent, but there are several participants in this study that demonstrate substantially higher competency than the rest of the sample.

The selected participants in this study *are exemplars in the field* of global leadership development with scores well above the norm on five competencies. Table 10 and Table 11 (parts 1 and 2) report the descriptive statistics for this sample in the GLTAP competencies, including the *Social Desirability* measure, which was a selection criterion.

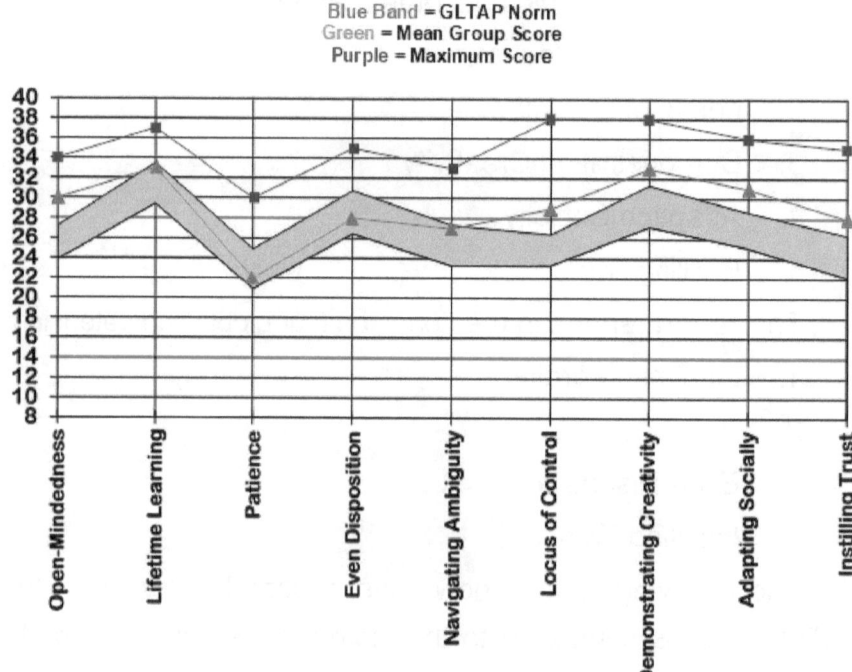

Global Leader TAP Profile
Blue Band = GLTAP Norm
Green = Mean Group Score
Purple = Maximum Score

Figure 12

Highest reported score for competencies.

Note. The thicker band represents the mean and one standard deviation, calculated as .5 of a standard deviation on either side of the mean. This mean was determined by 1,880 global leaders as part of the validation of the GLTAP.

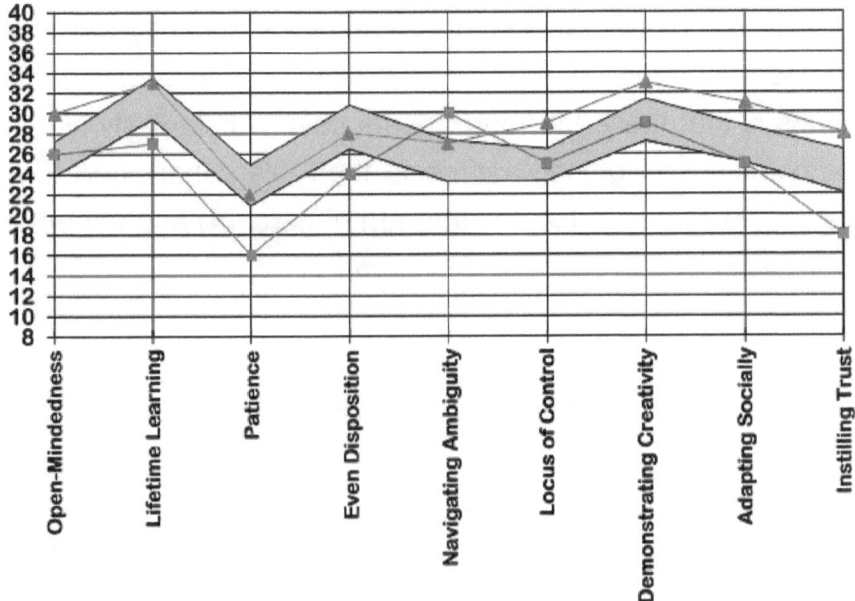

Global Leader TAP Profile
Blue Band = GLTAP Norm
Green = Mean Group Score
Red = Minimum Score

Figure 13. Lowest reported score for competencies.

Note. The thicker band represents the mean and one standard deviation, calculated as .5 of a standard deviation on either side of the mean. This mean was determined by 1,880 global leaders as part of the validation of the GLTAP.

In reporting the GLTAP competency data, a scattergram of the participants shows that all competencies clustered roughly in the 25-32 area of the scale. There were several "breakout" participants who were significantly deviant in the positive direction, as Figure 15 shows. These participants will be the subject of additional research in the next chapter. An analysis was conducted to determine the extent to which this breakout group had any specific competency trends that were over or under the GLTAP standard deviations. In fact, there were four participants (Steven, John, Calvin, and Tjp) who showed substantially higher raw and net difference scores (in a positive direction) than their peers across the GLTAP results. What this means is that these four participants have substantially higher competencies in global leadership than this cohort, and they are shown clearly in the scattergram (Figure 14) and the other analyses shown in Figures 15, 16, and 17.

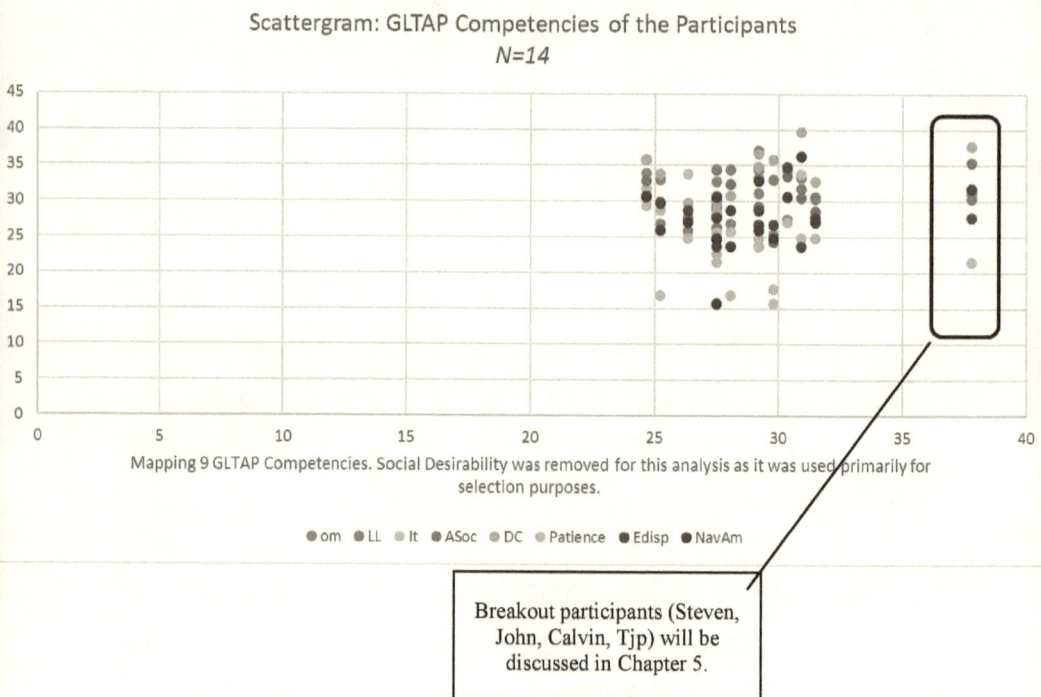

Figure 14. Scattergram of the GLTAP competencies.

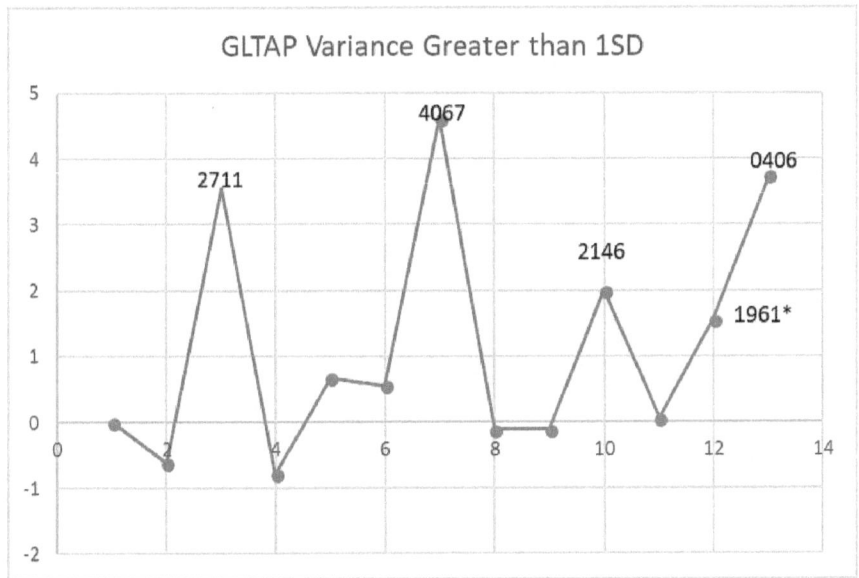

Figure 15. Over/Under GLTAP 1 SD.

Note. 1961 was removed from the study for not meeting the Caligiuri 10 Tasks selection criterion. This leader does not have a global role yet the participant's scores on the GLTAP indicate the leader would be more effective than the norm (of 698 leaders across 9 nationalities) were the leader to be appointed to a global role.

The over/under analysis led to viewing the Net Effect of GLTAP differences from the global norms. This analysis collected the differences between the individual participant's GLTAP score from the global norm, at the top or bottom of the standard deviation of the norm and plotting it on a graph. The four male participants showed substantially higher competence than their peer group, as can be seen by Figure 16.

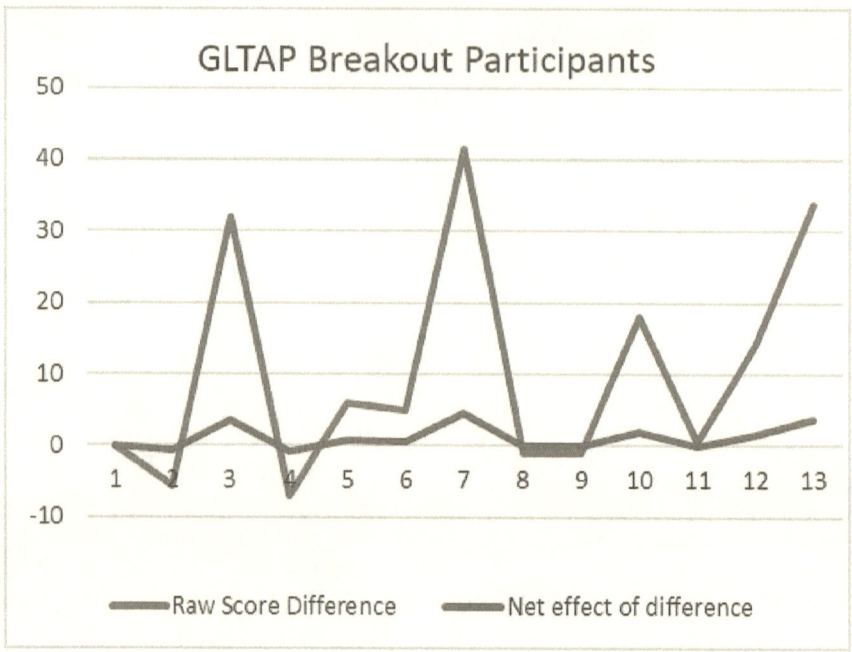

Figure 16. Net effective difference scores from the GLTAP norms.

Note. This chart clearly identifies subjects 2711, 4067, 2146, and 0406 which are male. Subject 1961 was removed from the analysis and reported results due to failing the selection criterion.

Table 10

Descriptive Statistics for the GLTAP (4 variables)

	des	loc	om	LL
Mean	26.41275983	28.89790571	30.13311786	32.95239836
Standard Error	0.546757002	0.869546413	0.788183669	0.808125955
Median	26.666664	28.5714	30.666475	33.9999915
Mode	27.556	27.428544	27.19983	34.666658
Standard Deviation	2.045777376	3.253544761	2.949113247	3.023730448
Sample Variance	4.185205074	10.58555351	8.697268944	9.142945825
Kurtosis	-0.715369125	3.489552416	-1.437454947	0.135037645
Skewness	0.054012622	1.433746897	-0.154428112	-0.833870178
Range	7.1111104	13.143248	8.53316	10.666664
Minimum	23.1111088	24.571	25.59984	26.66666
Maximum	30.2222192	37.714248	34.133	37.333324
Sum	369.7786376	404.57068	421.86365	461.333577
Count	14	14	14	14
Confidence Level(95.0%)	1.18119669	1.878540817	1.702767294	1.745849983

Des = Social Desirability   Om = Open-Mindedness

Loc = Locus of Control   LL = Lifetime Learning

Table 11

Descriptive Statistics for the GLTAP (6 variables)

	It	ASoc	DC	Patience	Edisp	NavAm
Mean	28.42857143	30.76921257	33.92857	22.44791429	28.14286	27.99862857
Standard Error	1.252313401	0.81854484	0.898499	1.171384966	0.769309	1.332690196
Median	28	30.461408	34.5	23.4275	28	27.4272
Mode	34	29.538432	35	25.1416	28	30.8556
Standard Deviation	4.685727687	3.062714347	3.361874	4.38292121	2.878492	4.986470114
Sample Variance	21.95604396	9.380219173	11.3022	19.20999834	8.285714	24.8648842
Kurtosis	0.358358768	-0.159957295	-0.98949	-0.968523847	1.473246	1.640310728
Skewness	-0.499034194	-0.117913502	0.114527	-0.263266805	0.669006	-0.687006836
Range	17	11.076912	11	13.7138	11	20.5708
Minimum	18	24.61536	29	15.9992	24	15.9992
Maximum	35	35.692272	40	29.713	35	36.57
Sum	398	430.768976	475	314.2708	394	391.9808
Count	14	14	14	14	14	14
Confidence Level(95.0%)	2.705458619	1.768358616	1.941088	2.530623365	1.661992	2.879102127

It = Instilling Trust   Patience = Patience

ASoc = Adapting Socially   Edis = Even Disposition

DC = Demonstrating Creativity   Navam = Navigating Ambiguity

Results of the Actualized Leader Profile (ALP)

The ALP framework is based on several psychological theories related to this study: McClelland's motivation theory, Jung's theory of personality, and Maslow's theory of self-actualization. The psychometrically validated ALP is a 57-item self-report assessment that measures an individual's dominant motive need, corresponding leadership style and leadership "shadow," and the conception of self-actualization treated as a fourth motive need and a modifier of the first three motive needs.

A detailed analysis was conducted to compare the self-actualization scores from the ALP in context with the GLTAP and GBE results to identify any trends. A chart of the self-actualization scores relative to the GLTAP competencies was also prepared. This analysis (Figure 17) showed an interesting trend in social desirability, which remained relatively flat, while the self-actualization scores varied greatly. Therefore, further analysis would be useful to determine if this relationship remains consistent in future larger sample studies.

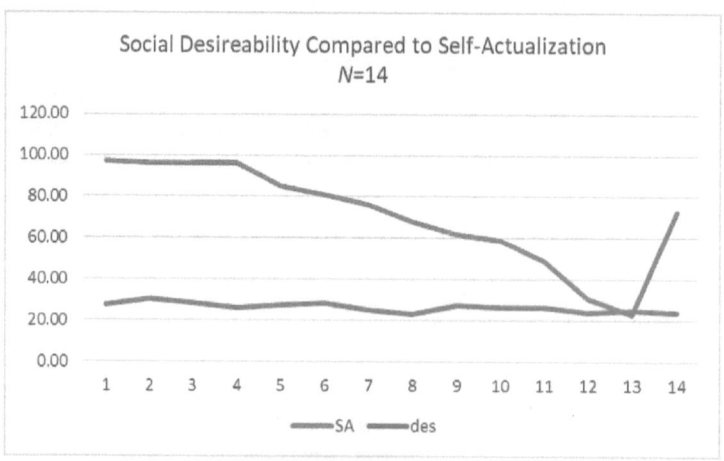

Figure 17. Social desirability compared to self-actualization measure.

A table completes this analysis by comparing results across the three psychometrics, ranking the participants by their ALP self-actualization scores from highest to lowest. The self-actualization scores range from 23 to 97, as shown by Table 12, which puts perspective on the self-actualization scores of participants while considering their reported episodes of TL across their lifespans.

Table 12

Self-Actualization (ALP) Comparison to GLTAP and GBE

Participant #	Pseudonym	ALP	GLTAP		GBE	
		Self-Actualization	Highest Above Average Competencies	Driving Performance	Building Team Effectiveness	Global Networking
0406	TJP	97	Open-mindedness, Navigating Ambiguity, Locus of Control, Demonstrating Creativity, Adapting Socially, Instilling Trust	19.5	18.3	19.0
3132	T. Rose	96	Demonstrating Creativity, Adapting Socially, Instilling Trust	18.5	18.3	17.5
1234	Pierre	96	Lifetime Learning; Demonstrating Creativity	17.5	17.5	18
3033	D. Lewis	96	Lifetime Learning; Patience; Even Disposition; Navigating Ambiguity; Locus of Control; Demonstrating Creativity; Adapting Socially	19	19	18
4067	J. Stephens	85	Open-Mindedness; Lifetime Learning; Patience; Even Disposition; Navigating Ambiguity; Locus of Control; Demonstrating Creativity; Adapting Socially	17.25	17.83	15
2711	S. Neeson	81	Open Mindedness; Navigating Ambiguity; Locus of Control; Demonstrating Creativity; Adapting Socially; Instilling Trust	18.5	18	18
4324	Berg	76	Lifetime Learning, Navigating Ambiguity	14.5	16.33	17.5
1961	T. Jelly	73	Demonstrating Creativity, Lifetime Learning, Adapting Socially, Open-Mindedness, Locus of Control	18	16.5	19
0594	J. Powers	68	Instilling trust	17.5	16.33	17.5
2210	B. Spence	62	Open Mindedness, Instilling Trust	16	15.17	15
2355	Lincs	59	Open Mindedness; Locus of Control; Demonstrating Creativity; Instilling Trust	17.5	17	15.5
0909	J. Rugby	49	Lifetime Learning; Adapting Socially	17.25	17.5	16.5
2508	O. Welch	31	Lifetime Learning; Adapting Socially	11.25	16.5	19
2146	C. Anderson	23	Open mindedness, Lifetime Learning, Patience, Navigating Ambiguity, Locus of Control, Demonstrating Creativity	20	17.67	19
1952	A. Thomas	0	0	19.25	19.25	20
3282	J. Schmalz	0	0	0	0	0

The sample's age demographic ranged from 42 to 63. During this period of an individual's career (e.g., later in career), it could be expected that the leader's self-actualization might be related to age. Analysis of the relationship between the age variable of this sample with the self-actualization and leader motivation style was conducted. As Table 13 illustrates, for this small sample, a significant relationship is noted between self-actualization and the "Achiever" motive profile, but not age. Future studies could provide a stronger analysis of age to self-actualization and motives of behaviors of leaders across the age span (early career, mid-career, and later career). For this study, no conclusions can be drawn on the age variable, but it suggests that additional research might prove useful.

Concerning the negative correlation of Self-Actualization to the Achiever style of Leadership, it would seem on the surface that the higher the level of a leader's role the higher the leader's self-actualization. During the interviews, what emerged instead was a sense of "loss of purpose" once the leaders had arrived at the highest levels of leadership and had all the financial security they could ever need. The leaders remarked that they were yearning for time off for themselves, and in some cases, the leaders have taken time off between companies to refocus their physical fitness regime or return to playing concert piano, for example. So, while McClelland's model suggests that the Achievement motivator, which is narrowly focused on achievement, helps to get to the top, it does not sustain an individual. The self-actualization, or sense of life purpose, prevails in driving the executive to other needs. What this small cohort data suggests is that older leaders may, in fact, be more driven by Affirming others (positive correlation of 0.161387491).

This phenomenon, which could be described as "making peace with one's purpose in life," would benefit from a further study into a larger sample to determine if these age-related motives move in the same directions. This would add value in understanding the motives of senior executive leaders, and it may provide ideas for how to continue the senior executive's development in ways other than philanthropy and boards of directors for other companies or not-for-profits.

Table 13

Age Correlation to ALP Self-Actualization and Motive Behaviors

	Age Calculation	Self-Actualization	Achiever	Affirmer	Asserter
Age Calculation (Ages 42-63)	1				
Self-Actualization	0.274378977	1			
Achiever	-0.375387924	-0.713067221	1		
Affirmer	-0.183992605	0.161387491	-0.392865402	1	
Asserter	0.440890641	-0.217611155	0.077538521	-0.294676252	1

Note. Only the "Achiever" motive leadership style appears to be correlated with self-actualization, albeit in an inverse way, indicating that high achievers are inversely correlated with self-actualization, as theorized by the ALP measure.

The self-actualized Achiever behavior pattern shows up in the life stories of the executives, as noted here:

Without wanting to give you a cliché, I do see that life is a journey and one where you have peaks and troughs on the way. I'm not the sort who sees it making towards a peak or whatever. I see it more like climbing in the Scottish mountains, where you climb up to and then down from one peak, and you go to the next one, and down, and then you go to the next one. I'm the type who will just get on with it. So, the pressure was on me, but I did extremely well. I think at the end of the year I had come, on most topics, in the top 3 in the top set. And I remember the headmaster—we used to get a written report—said something like, "I can't think why we even hesitated to put him in that top set." So, my dad was so proud, and I was because it was sort of vindication. They might have put me in it anyway after, but it was something important in proving myself right. (Lincs)

I'm an engineer, but my math teacher in high school said, "Have you thought this all the way through?" when I told her what my degree was going to be in. I mean, you know, she was just trying to, I think, she was generally concerned and says, "Look if your math skills. Do you know how hard that's going to be?" Yeah, you know, I'll figure it out. And, it was *that* hard. I made a C in four calculus classes in a row. C, C, C, C. I made a C, but I made it through four calculus classes, right? So, it's just part of my, I don't have to win everything, but I'll get through it. And you know, there was also an event in there where, you know, it was one of those deals, where like they picked the top, you know, leadership students from all the colleges in the country, like two from Kentucky, two from New York, two, two, two, two. It was like, you know, loading up Noah's Ark with college kids. So, but, I went to San Francisco and it was like an out of body experience that weekend. I met these people, who were like, you know, from a Utopian society I had never seen before, you know. We gallivanted around San Francisco and all of a sudden, and I remember in the check in line, there were people from Harvard and there were people from Penn, and there were people from UCLA. And, I'm thinking, what in the hell am I doing in this line? Where is the line for the people from the you know, the normal states? But same kind of deal. I'm, huh, funny enough, when you got in there and started having those conversations, you know, I can probably hang with most of those groups. I wouldn't want to, you know, square off necessarily with them on the SAT, but if it comes down to actually, you know, moving the ball in the real world, you know I came home going. Hmm, I could probably figure that out. You know, I worked really hard. You know, I took the jobs nobody else wanted. (John)

And so, like, huh, this kid! You throw him in. He kind of swims out the other end. . . They are like, "Holy crap! This guy who doesn't speak any Spanish, but yet he came out the other end with the objective!" (John)

My husband would say I have two speeds: 100% forward, and, asleep! (Rose)

And, I do it to you as if I was there now. I'll talk to the team about the Three-I's: Insight, Ideas, and Initiative that's consuming people. That's what I need from them all. Insight, ideas, and initiative. If you've got all three of those, you can really make stuff happen. In any one or two together, does not work. Not a good idea, and it's not based on a great insight is— it's kind of manufacturing centric, and if you get a great idea, but you're not taking the initiative to make it happen, then it's just hot air. (Jack)

I think, what you see is what you get with me. I hope you get a sense of that. (Lincs)

Nothing in my mind so far is a story of someone who's fallen into a career that actually they really, really are genuinely passionately interested about. So, it's been so much fun. There's been times when I can't believe they pay me to do it. (Berg)

That's when I decided to leave. It was kind a big turning point there. Why would anyone leave when you're on that trajectory? [Interviewer]: Yeah. Well, as you pointed out, what is the answer. Why would they? [Participant] Because it no longer feeds your soul. If you're not feeding something other than just your paycheck, it's no longer in alignment with what you're doing. Then you're in the wrong place. I mean. If you dread getting up every day going to work, you're doing the wrong thing. You could be make a million dollars a year but if dread every day and your blood pressure is up. When the phone rings you don't want to answer it because you don't want to face the conversation. You don't want to check your email and feel in trepidation when you do. You're in the wrong place. (Lincs)

The Overcomer "Achiever Leader." The type being described by the ALPs Achiever profile could also be labeled, the *Overcomer*, or someone who overcomes all the odds. As an example, John noted the annual viewing of a movie to remind himself of his modest roots and his aspirational goals. The movie, "Rudy," portrays a young man from the wrong side of the tracks that won't take no for an answer. This movie shows how, through hard work and intrinsic motivation, this young man succeeded in attending Notre Dame on scholarship and playing in the varsity football team. The movie was released in 1993 by U.S. director, David Anspaugh. For a YouTube trailer of this movie, please click here: https://www.youtube.com/watch?v=eDKOIH0I0nQ

How money motivates. A significant issue confronting many of these executives was the early realization that they needed to apply themselves to hard work to break through the socioeconomic levels into which they were born. Often mentioned in the interviews was the drive to keep earning more and rising higher in the organization's hierarchy to avoid "turning out like my parents," who later in life had no financial security. Many of these executives were not only supporting their children, but also both sets of parents. An example of this phenomenon is captured by John:

To end up in the same spot where both of my parents and my in-laws did, which is, they kind of got to one point in life and they had it all kind of lined up, and then it kind of melted underneath them right, which is I think a lot worse than if you say you were lower middle class and you were always lower middle class and you were always struggling. [. . .] I don't want to end up that way. (John)

This Achiever motive profile is consistent with behaviors described by the ALP model, as defined by its publisher (Sparks & Repede, 2016):

Achievers, those with a high need for achievement, are driven for success, improvement, and accomplishment. They are primarily concerned with expertise and competence, and are detail-oriented, focused, and very well-organized. These individuals are efficient, rules and process-oriented, and prefer consistency and predictability. Under stress, however, their Leadership Shadow triggers, and Achiever becomes narrow-minded and rigid, transforming into the classic "micromanager." (p. 27).

The Achiever behavioral profile has a concomitant Leadership Shadow described best as a "Fear of Failure." This pattern is typically induced more quickly under stress, during which the leader exhibits narrow-minded, inflexible, obsessive, argumentative, and pessimistic patterns. An example of this pattern would be a thinking-feeling-acting shadow cycle as shown in Table 14.

Table 14

The "Shadow" of the "Achiever"–Motivated Leader Style

Thoughts	Feelings	Behaviors
I have to always be perfect.	Inadequate	Becoming obsessive and nitpicky.
No one else can do this as well as me.	Frustration	Being overly critical and micromanaging.
I am not enough; I have to earn love.	Worthlessness	Taking on too many projects or staying overscheduled.

(Sparks & Repede, 2016; cited with permission of the publisher, Sparks Associates, Inc.)

Interestingly enough, however, the Group ALP Profile reports that the mean values of the ALP for this group is the Asserter profile. Including their leadership sequences, shadow (extent to which stress provokes their less pleasant thoughts, feelings, and behaviors), the most dominant leadership motivator profiles this group as Asserters with firm resistance to stress with the exception of a moderate amount of stress provoking a fear of betrayal. The results of the ALP, GLTAP, GBE, and the Caligiuri Scale all provide a backdrop to the life story interviews.

In summary, the selection process was effective in admitting only the highest quality global leaders, as measured by the Caligiuri Scale, the GLTAP, and the GBE, into a study. The McAdams interview protocol was a useful tool in provoking reflections and drawing out stories of the types of experiences that had a transformative effect on the identity formation of individual leaders. Many leaders shared a global storyline of progressive success followed by an awakening caused by a sudden departure from expectations, a similar deontology, and similarity in motive drivers and leadership style, as measured by the ALP.

CHAPTER FIVE

---✕•◦◉◦•✕---

Significance of the Findings

This study claims that developmental learning is linked to meaning construction in foreseeable ways throughout the lifespan. Evidence in the life story narratives of the study subjects provides justification of this. The study results using the McAdams Life Story Interview offers contributions for the leadership literature, as it exposes the antecedents and the trigger events of change, self-reflection, descriptions of self-concepts, and the depiction of leadership in action. As was suggested by Turner and Mavin (2008), further research into the experience of isolation and vulnerability, as well as how emotions impact the performance of leaders in their roles was possible with this interview format. The most significant reason to study the emotional side of leaders is to examine their process of becoming one's own person. Interpreting Jung, King and Nicol (1999) suggested that, "[t]he individuation process occurs as one's ego is initially developed, then challenged, and ultimately subordinated to a more comprehensive psychic entity, the Self," which "becomes the seat of one's identity" (p. 236).

Although the number of participants was not sizeable, it provided significant direction for answers to the research question. There is no doubt that future studies would benefit from a more significant number of women leaders in global leadership roles, as well as a better mix of nationalities and could be said to have limitations with regard to gender and national origin (Southeast Asian, South American, Middle East, or African leaders).

The leadership literature fails to fully explore the vulnerability leaders feel and how they manage their emotions in the context of their lives. This study examined the ways in which leaders handled significant emotional events, such as the death of a spouse, the loss of a significant position of power and prestige in a C-suite management role when the executive was terminated from the company after an acquisition, and a variety of other significantly challenging life events. This study contributes rare insight into the leader's emotional state during significant life changes.

Another contribution of this research study to the leadership literature is an examination of when and how becoming a leader occurs across the lifespan—a process deeply rooted in identity and consciousness much more than a construct with an outcome or a necessary "end point" to be achieved (Turner & Mavin, 2008, p. 389). In short, the leaders in this study describe leadership as a process which is both an ontology and a deotonology. The character traits and personalities that these executives used to adapt to the challenges in both their personal and business lives, which is usually presented as an idealized leadership model, has been contextualized. The study clearly provides significant examples of the executive's "personal goals and motives, defense mechanisms and coping strategies, mental representations of self and other, values and beliefs, developmental tasks and stage-related concerns, domain-specific skills and interests, and other personal characteristics that are contextualized in time, place, or social role" (McAdams, 2001, p. 111). As a result, this study responds to the McAdams call for making ongoing contributions to the personality literature, especially within psychology's newest branch of narrative identity psychology (McAdams, 2001).

The study links the transformative learning literature with identity (and identity literature) by describing how these executives found meaning and purpose in their lives and how they constructed and internalized their conscious awareness of who they are and how what they do for a living is an expression of their inner drives and desires for purpose. Through the study of the executives' identities, this study contributes evidence of their consciousness and how it relates to itself and world.

A potential criticism of the narrative methodology is the likelihood that in the process of telling one's story, some new awareness may emerge, perhaps suggesting that the life story interview itself may be somewhat of a trigger or a transformative experience (in and of itself). To answer this criticism, as is common in all IRB-approved studies of human subjects, a list of locally available psychological resources was available to the study participants after the study. Careful field notes documented the interviewer's impressions, reactions, and other significant events that may have occurred during or after the interview and noted possible adverse responses. Since the nature of the narrative reflects "ego development, personal adjustment, stress-related growth, and maturity, but not necessarily an immediate sense of subjective well-being," Singer (2004) suggests that acceptance of what "will never be . . . may allow for better long-term adjustment and more judicious life choices that leads to greater happiness in the long run" (p. 446). The issue of triggering a life transition following this interview is, therefore, a lessened concern. Survey research with these

16 participants 6 to 9 months after the interview would yield a definitive response to this criticism. It is beyond the scope of this dissertation to include this protocol at this time. However, all participants requested their transcripts, assessment reports, and a copy of the study. This provides an ongoing contact with participants to evaluate the effects of this process on their lives.

There is some evidence that the form of the interview may have an impact on the quality of the narrative. In one case, a study showed that written versus oral storytelling had a discernable difference in quality (Bohn & Berntsen, 2008). For gender, Bohn and Berntsen's study documented that women's stories were often longer than men's stories. Reasons for both criticisms are unknown. McAdams does not prescribe which method of collecting the data is preferred. Therefore, this study used an oral interview method and provided the typed transcripts to the participants. Only one participant provided edits to the transcript, and those changes were primarily typographical.

It is potentially bothersome to psychologists that this work lacks an organizing principle (other than time), and that the descriptions provided may be focused on the "cognitive and conscious aspects of personality at the expense of the irrational, affective and unconscious factors that shape individuals and their behavior" (Singer, 2004, p. 440). Since the "narrative memories . . . [are an account] of the individual's goal pursuits, obstacles, and outcomes" (p. 441) it is interesting to note that the storyline is embedded in a schema and an actual script that describes the event within a living story, giving it both historicity and meaning. It is also intriguing that the storyline may change, upon reflection on the experience. The study is describing conscious awareness and making note of any negative consequences in the life path which might be indicative of unresolved, shadow, or unconscious factors influencing the life path. It is beyond the scope of this study to examine those unconscious factors, but collecting both psychometric data via the ALP as well as story data via the McAdams interview would allow for future analysis and reporting of the unconscious factors that shape identity.

This study provides poignant examples which illustrate Newman's (2012) description of the effects of consciousness development. Each of this study's participants explained the perspective that transformed through difficult, at times heartbreaking, stories of being alone with their experience of loss or decision points through which they held their own counsel even from their spouses. Each of these transformations changed the person from the inside out, and the changes caused each individual to adapt consciously through significant reflection to find a new meaning that permitted each one to continue his/her life and career progress. These leaders did not have an easy time of these transformations. In many cases, transformation had a significant effect on their internalized sense of themselves and where they stood within the social milieu they had created for themselves.

This study shows the continuity of consciousness development across a unified storyline of each executive's life. In this study we see how their perspective evolved and how their values were reinforced across all types of situations from the grade school playground, through their college years, into their early careers, in establishing a family and becoming a parent, to burying their loves ones even during the time their proverbial "stars were ascending" in their corporate careers.

Their life stories have shown how identity grows from the inside out, and then how individuals choose to show this identity with a mask of who they want to be for purposes of self-preservation in the work world. Remarkably, those masks developed in their adolescence and the freedom to express themselves (for who they really are, authentically) was a constant thread throughout the life of these global leaders. As Erikson (1950) described, their core personality development was a constant golden thread throughout their life stories, and in the telling of their stories, it seemed important for them to bring attention to it.

From the perspective of developmental psychology, the drive to "become" who these subjects believed they should be and to have a more complete sense of themselves often exposed these executives to experiences that could not be accommodated in their existing meaning schemas. This realization was described as early as childhood and continued through late career stages of life in their stories of specific events that acted as triggers which challenged their habits of mind. This study traced these triggers which began the transformation through the disorienting dilemmas (Mezirow & Associates, 2000). The study provides evidence of the changes in consciousness and the perspective shifts that left them with a renewed sense of how to make their way in the world, fully cognizant of how to manage these life events in the context of a changed perspective of what that challenge meant to them. There were also many sudden and immediate epiphanies that traced the clearly outlined steps of Mezirow's (2000) 10-step process. The identification and description of these events and their antecedents is one of the significant contributions of this study. A gap had existed in understanding the life history of adult leaders who performed global leadership roles in multinational organizations. This study contributes important life story narratives to address this gap.

In the early stages of designing this study, a significant question was understanding how transformative learning affects identity, and whether TL and identity are, in fact, the same phenomenon. By studying the life experiences of these global leaders, a longitudinal description of the meaning these leaders made of their experiences across their lifespan came into view. The life stories contain the descriptions of what accounts for their unusual ability and capacity to withstand complex, demanding, challenging, ambiguous professional experiences as they navigate multinational decisions, people, and processes in their organizations. The answer lies in how they were taught how to handle responsibility during their childhood, and through this they developed a stable moral code that strengthened their inner resolve to live through the lens of their values and morals, even during stressful, significant transformative events in their lives.

This study also explored the linkage of TL as defined by Kegan (1994) to the development of GL as defined by Osland et al. The study provides a line of sight from case to case of the stages of intercultural competence (worldview, social interpersonal style, and situational approach) that developed through experience and how participants' cognitive abilities (personality and motives) developed over time (Kegan, 1994). By examining the lifeline, of each executive, the role that time plays becomes clear in preparing these executives for increasingly complex and challenging roles and responsibilities.

Cumberland et al. (2016) proposed that effective assessment practices are the answer to identifying, selecting, and developing the prospective global talent in an organization. This study applied a protocol of assessments to determine what could be learned about the leaders' styles, dispositions, motives, values, and beliefs. This study group represents the 21st century global leader initially proposed theoretically (Heams & Harvey, 2006). Leaders in the new century are described as introspective, thoughtful, hard-working, generous, kind people. In a word, they have perseverance and humility. They understand their place in the world, they are grateful for the fruits of their labors, and they use their positions to give back to society in small and large ways, quietly.

This research was designed to help address questions about identity development and transformative experiences through the lifespan. This study provides answers to what constitutes a transformative experience in the life of a global leader. The study provides the descriptions of identity changes as they occurred through the life of the leader. The participants were conscious of the transformative events as they were occurring and the impact it was having on their lives. It is clear now that there are only a few *markers* that matter in the development of a global leader. Those *markers* contribute significantly to the successful journey across one's life from early childhood to late adulthood.

Further research may help to determine which of these markers are "nature" (i.e., intrinsic to the personality and character of the leader), versus "nurture" (e.g., a direct result of the upbringing, parenting, or mentoring) the executive received throughout the lifespan. This small study does not contain sufficient data to empirically separate the events from the people involved in sufficient depth to know whether the leader would have developed these same traits and beliefs in another setting. However, the subjects of this study came from entirely different walks of life, different countries of origin, different parental structures (some were orphaned and raised by an adopted family), and they were both male and female. All that can be said is that for this study at this time in history it appears that these leaders would have developed these same traits and dispositions without regard for nationality or country of origin. No challenge seemed too difficult to surmount for these leaders, and while it cannot be generalized, at least directionally speaking, it is likely that most global leaders share this inner drive to succeed and to do so on their own terms on a global scale. Life happens, and they make the most of it.

The Markers of Successful Global Leaders

The research question inherently suggests that life experiences could be related to, or actually be, the developmental process by which leaders develop an ability to navigate the complexity of multinational leadership roles. Is this true? In short, yes. The other part of the story is that individuals seeking global management roles also must bring to the experience(s) a set of personality characteristics, beliefs, values, and philosophy. To be successful in a multinational senior leadership position, individuals must possess an unwavering moral compass that allows them to walk away from individuals and groups who significantly challenge their morality. This set of critical factors may identify star performers who can pivot to top management roles, and when compared to the rest of the talent pool, may well identify those who are a best fit for global leadership responsibilities. The set of a markers, or a priori factors, can be summarized as shown in Table 15 and represents the single answer to the research question.

Table 15

Korver Model of Potential Capacity to Lead Globally (Markers)

A Priori Selection Factors for Global Leadership Roles (e.g. *Markers*)	Life Experience Criteria for Selection (*Experience Markers*)
• Can elucidate a deontological framework that includes factors of responsibility, self-awareness, desire to make the world a better place, high morality, strong moral compass in the face of peer pressure, transparent communication (open and honest), and belief in hard work. • Can describe a significant mentor or strong older person figuring prominently in their early life development (father, mother, uncle, aunt, neighbor, teacher, etc.). • Can describe a theater/movie, book, or family story that clearly portrays a moral story. This most likely will be related to their own life experience and will serve to narrate critical identity issues to be or already are resolved. (Also, a tendency to enjoy returning to this story over and over again at different times of life.) • Open mindedness about other places and peoples. • Truly values people. • Evidence of emotional intelligence.	• Desire to leave the provincial homeland. • Experiences of early leadership in different phases of life (typically rising to the top of the group, class, or sport). • Strong work ethic developed by paid employment starting at least in adolescence (age 12) if not sooner. • Evidence of philanthropy for social causes behind the scenes (volunteering or quiet money). • Can tell a story with a moral from any stage of life and the values expressed will be clear and compelling. • Stories of being 100% commercially available to their jobs, often making paradoxical choices between family and work. • Stories of being determined to figure out problems. Takes on the tough cases. Works harder than others. Often expects the same from their teams.

• Mature self-awareness at an early age. • A strong faith in themselves and a higher power. Spiritual, but not necessarily religious. • Sees money as security for the future, not a way of keeping score. • Politically liberal about social issues and fiscally conservative.	

Note: The psychometric *markers* are: (a) The top five competencies of Global Leaders (as measured by the GLTAP); (b) GBE over 15; (c) high self-actualization scores and Achiever and Asserter leader styles reported by the ALP.

Two factors stand out as quite paradoxical: Six participants had strong Catholic backgrounds, but no matter the religious affiliations of their youth, most had not continued a set of religious practices by mid-career. Instead, they described being deeply spiritual. The second paradox was their political philosophy: All participants were socially liberal, expressing the importance of caring for the less fortunate in society, no matter which country they were from nor in which country they currently lived (complete with examples of how they cared for the less fortunate themselves), and fiscally conservative with respect to government intervention or control.

A fundamental issue in the literature was where the ability to transform comes from, when it starts, and how does it work? This study makes an essential contribution to the understanding of transformative learning as it describes the earliest experiences of study subjects that were transformative, complete with the reflexive ability to consider the options, making tradeoff decisions that affected their social standing in their peer groups, and taking action that continued a consistent values-based thread from early life to adulthood. Clear and compelling evidence of transformative learning occurred as early as age 3 and continued throughout the lifespan.

This research sought to find the cultural and historical significance of the influences across the lifespan at this point in history. "This sensitivity to the nuances of sociocultural context prevents the privileging of a dominant ideological position, masquerading as an 'objective' scientific principle" (Singer, 2004, p. 439). When considering objectivity another way—regarding the role of the interviewer—there is potential bias in that a relationship may form between researcher and the subject, which could affect objectivity and may bias the analysis. The study attempts to minimize this with the use of a second coder. There is certainty that the relationship that developed not only increased the likelihood of honest responses based on the trust developed, but also that the inherent non-verbal communication guided the appropriate coding of themes with a more significant and more holistic (and hence, accurate) understanding of the subject. The interviewer also became a subjective participant in the interview process through attentional focus and verbal and non-verbal cues. The researcher took substantive field notes to record experiences that might indicate that the interview was biased positively or negatively in any way by the interviewer. There were no adverse findings. A relationship does develop between interviewee and interviewer, and for the life story interview, that is a positive and expected contribution to the very intimate nature of sharing one's

Promising Future Research

This study is the foundational work of a global leadership research program aimed at providing accurate ways of identifying potential global leaders and providing the right types of developmental activities to further the leader's success at scale in global organizations. With that program in mind, multiple study avenues offer promising future research. These are described below.

Predictive Model of Potential Capacity to Lead Globally

The proposed model of potential capacity to lead globally now serves as a set of *markers* that would be enhanced with a large-scale study of leaders at different stages of life, beginning with high school and college students with an interest in international trade or travel, early career employees or MBA students with an interest in expatriate work, and mid-career leaders on the succession track for placement in significant global leadership positions in multinational organizations. A survey-based study would serve to create a psychometrically sound set of measures for different stages of life, career stages, and experiences across the lifespan, resulting in a specific global leadership pipeline model.

Self-Actualization and Social Desirability: A Paradox That Needs More Study

Two very well-known concepts and well-respected measures are self-actualization and social desirability (i.e., response bias). Despite the low sample size (n=14), a significant correlation was found between self-actualization and social desirability. A correlation matrix (Pearson's r values) for the ALP measure of self-actualization and the 10 competencies in the GLTAP is provided in Table 16. At a 95% confidence level, .44 shows significance in a study of this size. As can be seen from Table 16, self-actualization and social desirability, as measured by the ALP and GLTAP, are positively correlated at .539. Self-Actualization and Demonstrating Creativity are also correlated at .511. Patience is negatively correlated with Self-Actualization. The Locus of Control measure is correlated at .496 with Self-Actualization. A future study with a much larger sample of ALP and GLTAP administrations would be helpful to understand the significance of the relationships between the ALP self-actualization measures and the GLTAP measures, possibly to refine a set of measures of significance for predicting success among global leaders at different stages of the lifespan.

Table 16

Pearson r GLTAP Competencies and ALP Self-Actualization

z	SA	des	loc	om	LL	It	ASoc	DC	Patience	Edisp	NavAm
SA	1										
des	0.539222	1									
loc	0.088957	0.283421	1								
om	-0.15176	0.012147	0.144143	1							
LL	-0.15758	-0.04632	-0.17703	0.269897	1						
It	0.228217	0.440237	0.099664	0.187052	-0.25544	1					
ASoc	0.050842	0.382801	0.325735	0.324219	0.224931	0.435401	1				
DC	0.511495	0.355104	0.496583	0.366201	0.299812	0.163236	0.367792	1			
Patience	-0.07074	0.109596	0.024139	0.411692	0.031593	0.646962	0.398985	0.266356	1		
Edisp	0.231771	0.552358	-0.10393	-0.27547	0.112785	0.411441	0.300703	0.024982	0.353361	1	
NavAm	0.402283	0.367728	0.331284	0.543604	0.069962	0.485358	0.162932	0.63714	0.319491	0.189858	1

Note: The significance of the relationship between Social Desirability and Self-Actualization can be seen clearly by Figure 17.

One hypothesis for this finding may be that these outstanding global leaders are operating at Kegan's Level 4 (Self-Authoring) of mental complexity, and are therefore still concerned with how they are showing up for others. At Kegan's Level 5 (Self-Transforming) of mental complexity, it would be expected that social desirability would fall away as a defining measure of the global leader's self-actualization. There never has been any analysis of these measures in an extensive study. Therefore, a promising area of potential interest would be to draw a larger study sample to compare the scores of global leaders on these two leadership indicators.

The Age-Related Motivators of the Senior Global Leader

The negative correlation between self-actualization and the achievement motivator was surprising and suggests that a larger cohort would help to determine if this was an anomaly or a trend. Further research would be valuable with different age groups to determine when, in fact, the changes in motivators emerge across the lifespan. Segregating senior executives in the cohort and expanding the number of participants in that demographic set would provide useful information from which to posit a theory.

The "Uber" Global Leader

Figures 14-17 reported participants with GLTAP scores significantly above the norms of the instrument. For the highest GLTAP competencies, an analysis of the 9 competencies compared to the Actualized Leader Profile's *Self-Actualization Scale* was conducted for initial comparison. The point of this analysis was to examine the extent to which self-actualization may relate in any way to competence as a global leader. This very preliminary analysis suggests that more study of the relationship between self-actualization and global competency would be beneficial with a larger population of global leaders. It would also be useful to examine these four participants' narratives more closely to determine any trends related to their self-actualization.

Questioning the Importance of Language Skills

Many of the participants' lowest scoring item on the Caligiuri Scale was Item #21, "I may need to speak in a language other than my mother tongue at work." Forty-six percent (46%) of the study participants were below a "4" on language, however even with this variable as a low score, it did not cause any participant to be removed from the study. It would be useful to determine the significance of this variable. A correlation analysis of the Caligiuri Scale using sample data was conducted and shown by Table 17. Item #21 is abbreviated as "Language." For this small sample, the correlation for language is significant with six of the Caligiuri Scale (10 global leader tasks). If a larger study of global leaders who have already taken the GLTAP and GBE are administered the Caligiuri survey as designed for this study, we may learn a great deal more about how language skills appear to predict success (the GLTAP) or how the experience of global leaders (GBE) maps onto the Caligiuri Scale. With descriptive statistics about the importance of language skills correlated with the GBE and GLTAP scales, it would be beneficial for determining the usefulness of using the Caligiuri Scale at all when identifying leaders for global roles. For purposes of the current study, language seems useful (correlated at .97 to .99) to external and internal clients, supervising multinational employees, implementing strategy, budgeting, negotiating, and dealing with suppliers and vendors, as well as managing risk. Separately, an analysis of whether North American executives score differently than the Asian, Eastern or Western European, or South American executives about how language skills affect success outcomes would be useful.

Table 17

Full Sample Correlations for the Caligiuri Global Leader Tasks

	Colleagues	Clients	Intl Clients	Language	Supervise	Strategy	Budget	Negotiate	Suppliers/Vendors	Risk
Colleagues	1									
Clients	0.243658	1								
Intl Clients	0.761639	0.172747	1							
Language	0.394771	0.275291	0.08583	1						
Supervise	1	0.243658	0.761639	0.394771	1					
Strategy	0.664292	-0.05245	0.334908	-0.01133	0.664292	1				
Budget	0.597695	-0.07938	0.275645	-0.01128	0.597695	0.951747	1			
Negotiate	0.281963	0.766462	0.199904	0.424083	0.281963	0.01821	-0.02901	1		
Suppliers/Vendors	-0.05941	0.686465	0.102429	0.134066	-0.05941	-0.39288	-0.39116	0.641956	1	
Risk	0.161861	0.552141	0.141011	0.332482	0.161861	-0.03122	0.003553	0.888129	0.495391	1

Successful Outcomes of Business Experience

International assignments continue to be the most popular method for developing global skills in executives. It would be highly useful to discern the relationship between the success predictors, as measured by the GBE, with the tasks performed by the global leaders in this sample (Caligiuri). A correlation between the Global Business Experience (GBE) survey and the Caligiuri 10 Tasks of Global Leaders was analyzed, finding significant relationships between tasks and the outcomes by the very experienced leaders in this very small study, suggesting that a larger study would help to create a better understanding of the predictive quality of these two measures for selection (see Table 18). The importance of this analysis was to validate that the tasks the leader performs are likely to produce the types of outcomes described in the Global Business Experience survey. Directionally, this appears to be correlated, which provides another follow-up study opportunity. Several factors have a significant relationship. Those are shown in Table 18.

Table 18

Correlation of the GBE and Caligiuri 10 Tasks of Global Leaders.

GBE	Pearson r (*N*=14)
Strategy and Budget	0.951747
Negotiation and Risk	0.888129
Colleagues, Supervision with International Clients and Negotiating With Internal Clients	.76 range

Table 19

Correlation of Caligiuri Scale and GBE (Pearson r)

	Driving	Building	Networking	Colleagues	Clients	Intl Clients	Language	Supervise	Strategy	Budget	Negotiate	Suppliers/Vendors	Risk
Driving	1												
Building	0.595537345	1											
Networking	0.209506444	0.436586827	1										
Colleagues	-0.079344019	0.130461542	0.080178373	1									
Clients	-0.1154282	-0.013897263	0.421654133	0.243657962	1								
Intl Clients	-0.336722362	0.034591178	-0.130362898	0.761639375	0.172747	1							
Language	0.322977155	0.25673576	0.293111613	0.394771017	0.275291	0.08583	1						
Supervise	-0.079344019	0.130461542	0.080178373	1	0.243658	0.761639	0.394771	1					
Strategy	-0.110927028	-0.013355334	-0.062138787	0.664291572	-0.05245	0.334908	-0.01133	0.664292	1				
Budget	0.043536322	0.21167069	0.122816959	0.597694624	-0.07938	0.275645	-0.01128	0.597695	0.951747	1			
Negotiate	-0.006333271	-0.224547584	0.295072762	0.281962951	0.766462	0.199904	0.424083	0.281963	0.01821	-0.02901	1		
Suppliers/Vendors	-0.231738595	-0.206319047	0.323413198	-0.059406057	0.686465	0.102429	0.134066	-0.05941	-0.39288	-0.39116	0.641956	1	
Risk	0.205180571	-0.051002391	0.291912204	0.161860619	0.552141	0.141011	0.332482	0.161861	-0.03122	0.003553	0.888129	0.495390619	1

The Significance of the Findings

Significance of the Findings for the Literature

Mezirow (2000) claimed the notion that TL is only an adult phenomenon, while Erickson (2007) posited that some form of identity development occurs early in life, and Newman (2012) and Illeris (2014) suggested that identity cannot *only* be an adult manifestation. This study makes a contribution to TL theory by providing data of transformative experiences earlier than adulthood. Through this study, Mezirow's theory of TL has provided a process for viewing life stories, while Kegan's theories helped frame the outcomes or the stopping points between the transformative stages.

Personality psychologists, particularly those who are narrative identity theorists, have an interest in how people make meaning across their lives, and in this study how global leaders make meaning from their experiences was uncovered. Another area of interest was how global leaders achieved a self-defining narrative, and whether they made a career choice because of this self-definition during adolescence. As a result, this study offers a discovery equally relevant to TL, GL, and personality psychology. A contribution in the human development and human resource development literature can be made in response to the call by Turner and Mavin regarding a leader's subjective realities. This study contributes to how leaders develop across different parts of their careers and considers other factors not ordinarily observed by organizations other than the organizational life of the leader. This study describes the full extent of the impact of life challenges that attend to the maturing executive as he/she achieves senior executive roles.

The stage theorists and TL theorists might be interested in this study's report of when TL first occurred. This finding suggests that stage theory may benefit from being expanded, as well as the TL theory, to embrace some form of TL appearing earlier in life. This study shows which traits appear to matter for global leaders. This may interest personality theorists. The study shows what influenced the development of the person's meaning-making experiences at different stages of consciousness and age. Studying senior leaders, as we are in this study–especially those in global general management roles–gives us first-hand evidence of the types and nature of experiences in earlier life and provides some evidence of the executive's reflexive awareness. The study helps to answer to these questions by employing two personality instruments and viewing the leaders' stories with that lens.

Across the three primary literatures: TL, identity theory of personality development, and the global leadership literature, the question surrounding *what happens during a person's development across their lifespan, beginning in childhood, that might predispose him/her to success in roles that require significant cross-cultural, geographic, and temporal adjustments* has been addressed. This study's research sought to resolve the many gaps previously found in understanding identity development and transformative learning.

Significance of the Findings for the Central Research Question

What are the significant life events reported by global leaders of multinational organizations that could be related to their capacity in navigating the complexity of their roles? This study describes a trajectory, beginning with early work experience in adolescence, early leadership experiences in late adolescence and early adulthood, and the decision to leave their provincial homeland to accelerate their career. In the middle years, the development of a deontological framework that includes strong values in action, often supported and nurtured by a strong mentor, catapults the leader into development of open mindedness, a value of people, emotional intelligence, and mature self-awareness at an early age. These global leaders have a strong faith in themselves and they see money as security, not a license to brag. Finally, we see a socially liberal and fiscally conservative individual emerging with a desire to take on the tough-to-solve problems that allows them to work hard and feel satisfaction in their accomplishments. These leaders succeeded against all odds until they hit a wall, and experienced the "big fall," which repositioned and humbled them for consideration of how far up the career ladder they wanted to go. Many will choose to continue to the pinnacle role (CEO), while others will turn their attention from organizational achievement to satisfaction of intrinsic needs to complete themselves with music, travel, and family. All in all, the leaders share a remarkable consistency in their stories and remarkable resilience in living through extremely difficult life challenges.

Significance of the Findings for Leadership Development Practice

The 21st century provides an extraordinary opportunity to examine the intersection of several disciplines and scholarly pursuits. As organizations continue their global imperatives, employees at all levels of the organization will experience identity challenges. The work of intentionally changing people for the benefit of economic gain should be examined more openly for conscious development and intentional change, along with offering support for managing the significant emotional changes that attend visible growth of such an intimate nature.

This study provides a description of how certain life experiences are connected to the identity formation of leaders.

Leaders have a unique identity; that is, they are at the same time acting from their core values and employing behaviors developed across a lifetime of experiences, but they also have a larger responsibility to the people they lead and to the successful outcomes they are leading in their organizations. From a scholarly standpoint, Newman (2012) would say that our identity is our persona. As a leader, this is the mask or identity or persona that one shows the world. Our consciousness, by contrast, Newman describes as the "essence of our experience" (p. 394). Global leadership is one of the career paths that allows for the harmonizing of persona and consciousness, which uniquely allows the real person (inside and outside) to be one and the same. This type of work helps integrate or make more congruent the persona and consciousness. The congruence may be related to the intra-psychic demands of living in a different culture and communicating in a second language. Or, it just may be too much for the human brain to manage all the complexities, and the "mask" or persona falls away because much more significant challenges must be addressed for the leader to succeed. For success in leadership, managing this duality takes reflection and continuous feedback. This dilemma, of the duality of the leader's role, almost led to changing the research question to: *How does the transformative learning process develop the identity of the global leader?* This question suggested that research into whether a global leader is an identity and global leadership is a transformative process, or the outcome of that identity, would be worthwhile.

This study used a set of assessment practices that may create a baseline of developmental experiences needed for future success, as compared to experiences that an individual has already had. The antecedents, critical reflections, and conscious actions by leaders that appear as visible manifestations in their interviews, provide substantiation that they are prepared for the challenges of the next step in their global leadership role because of the role. By conducting a thorough interview-based assessment process, skilled executive assessors may refine their recommendations on which leaders should advance, based on this new and potentially significant success metric.

In addition to assessment, a useful tool for development is applying the rubric offered in Chapter 4, the Conscious/Unconscious-Wanted/Unwanted, 2 x 2 Framework (see Figure 1). This personal assessment for change is a large part of the work a global leader must undertake to understand himself/herself, and it contributes to a global leader being able to define his or her ontology, and then convert it into a deontology. That work, creating a personal leadership theory that defines a global leader's personal philosophy of leading, is crucial to his or her success. This deontology presents a set of boundary conditions or moral considerations that the leader can use to determine whether the actions he or she is taking as a leader are right or wrong. It also offers the leader a set of rules to live by rather than acting purely from a commercial point of view, which is antithetical to the real global leader's personal philosophy of life.

Significance of the Key Concepts

For those in the field of leadership development, the most significant finding from this study is the conclusion that the developmental experiences of leaders are *identity* development experiences. Few talent leaders lack awareness of the highly intimate nature of leadership development activities but understanding how it develops the individual's identity causes it to take on increased significance and suggests that additional support would be appropriate during the transformative process. This is where executive coaching can ensure success. Further, this study identifies how expatriate roles accelerate this identity work. Leadership development practitioners would be well advised to consider the impact of the work assignment, since it will never leave the executive where he or she started: It is a pivot to an entirely new realm of consciousness and behavior. These leaders cannot go home again and be the way they used to be, or said another way, re-entry may be problematic.

The sensitivity of this work needs more consideration for strategic talent management as it is not only developing the leader, but also affecting the leader's core identity, and as a result, the individual's family and life trajectory. In this case, the work of the leadership development professional is critical to achieving the goals of the organization while being highly sensitive to the profound personal changes the individual leader is undertaking. Few leaders enter the promotional track thinking about how it will change them. Perhaps more research in this area would be useful for both the practitioner and the leader.

Key Methodological Insights of the Study

The use of narrative (story) in the collection of data provides a rich trove for analysis. This study will afford many additional years of analysis leading to uncovering and refining the tools, models, and strategies for development of individual leaders at the intersection of transformative learning, leadership development, consciousness, and identity.

Significance of the Findings as the Newly Minted Scholar/ Practitioner/Global Leader

This study in many ways feels like trying to capture the in-between state of the caterpillar in the cocoon while transforming into a butterfly. While there are few scientific instruments to measure this human space of transformation from the inside out, it is nonetheless real and can be explained by those experiencing it. The study was ethno-biographical as it describes the life experiences of the researcher, who is herself a global leader. This modest contribution to the literature and practice of global leadership development, it is hoped, will enable those who enjoy a life of travel and managing significant challenges the opportunity they were born to achieve.

References

Anonomous. (n.d.).

Bazigos, M., Gagnon, C., & Schaniger, B. (2016, January). *Leadership in Context*. Retrieved from McKinsey Quarterly: http://www.mckinsey.com/business-functions/ organization/our-insights/leadership-in-context

Bohn, A., & Berntsen, A. (2008). Life story development in childhood: The development of life story abilities and the acquisition of cultural life scripts from late middle childhood to adolescence. *Developmental Psychology, 44*(4), 1135-1147. doi:10.1037/0012-1649.44.4.135

Caligiuri, P. (2006). Developing global leaders. *Human Resource Management Review, 16*, 219-228.

Caligiuri, P., & Tarique, I. (2009). Predicting effectiveness in global leadership activities. *Journal of World Business, 44*, 336-346. doi:10.11016.j.jwb.2008.11.005

Clark, M. C., & Dirkx, J. M. (2000). Moving beyond a unitary self: A reflective dialogue. In A. Wilson & E. Hayes (Eds.),. In *Handbook of Adult and Continuing Education*. San Francisco, CA: Jossey-Bass.

Cranton, P., & Kasl, E. (2012). A response to Michael Newman's "Calling transformative learning into question: Some mutinous thoughts". *Adult Education Quarterly, 62*(4), 393-398. doi:10.1177/0741713612456418

Cumberland, D. M., Herd, A., Alagaraja, M., & Kerrick, S. A. (2016). Assessment and development of global leadership competencies in the workplace: A review of literature.

Advances in Developing Human Resources, 18(3), 301-317.

Daloz, L. (2000). Transformative learning for the common good. In J. M. Associates (Ed.), *Learning as Transformation: Critical perspectives on a theory in progress* (pp. 103-123). San Francisco, CA: John Wiley & Sons.

Daloz, L. A. (1996). *Common Fire: leading lives of commitment in a complex world.* Beacon Press.

Dirkx, J. M. (2012). Self-formation and transformative learning: A response to "Calling transformative learning into question: Some mutinous thoughts," by Michael Newman. *Adult Education Quarterly, 62*(4), 399-405. doi:10.1177/0741713612456420

Dirkx, J. M., Mezirow, J., & Cranton, P. (2006, April). Musings and reflections on the meaning, context, and process of transformative learning: A dialogue between John M. Dirkx and Jack Mezirow. *Journal of Transformative Education, 4*(2), 123-139. doi:10.1177/1541344606287503

Dix, M. (2016). The cognitive spectrum of transformative learning. *Journal of Transformative Education, 14*(2), 139-162. doi:10.1177/1541344615621951

Erickson, D. M. (2007). A developmental re-forming of the phases of meaning in transformational learning. *Adult Education Quarterly, 58*(61), 61-80. doi:10.1177/0741713607305936

Erikson, E. H. (1950). *Childhood and society.* New York, NY: Norton.

Erikson, E. H. (1982). *The life cycle completed.* New York, NY: Norton.

Freire, P. (1970). *Pedagogy of the oppressed.* New York, NY: Seabury.

Freire, P. (1999). *Mentor.* San Francisco, CA: Jossey-Bass.

Gagnon, S. C. (2014). Rethinking global leadership development programmes: The interrelated significance of power, context and identity. *Organization Studies, 35*(5), 645-670. doi:10.1177/0170840613509917

Habermas, T., & Bluck, S. (2000). Getting a life: The emergence of the life story in adolescence. *Psychological Bulletin, 126*(5), 748-769. doi:10.1037/0033-2909.126.5.748

Heams, J. T., & Harvey, M. (2006). The evolution of the concept of the 'executive' from the 20th century manager to the 21st century global leader. *Journal of Leadership & Organizational Studies*, Vol 13, Issue 2, 29-41.

Henderson, J. (2002). *Transformative learning in the executive suite: CEOs and the role of context in Mezirow's theory.* (Doctoral dissertation): Retrieved from ProQuest Dissertations and Theses database. (UMI No. 3037824).

Hoggan, C. D. (2016). Transformative learning as a metatheory: Definition, criteria, and typology. *Adult Education Quarterly, 66*(1), 57-75. doi:10.1177/0741713615611216

Holt, K., & Seki, K. (2012). Global leadership: A developmental shift for everyone. *Industrial and Organizational Psychology, 5*(2), 196-215. doi:10.1111/j.1754-9434.2012.01431.x

Illeris, K. (2014). Transformative learning re-defined: As changes in elements of the identity. *International Journal of Lifelong Education, 33*(5), 573-586. doi:10.1080/02601 370.2014.917128

Illeris, K. (2015). Book Review: Transformative learning and identity. *Journal of Transformative Education, 13*(4), 366-369. doi:10.1177/1541344615589818

Jokinen, T. (2005). Global leadership competencies: A review and discussion. *Journal of European Industrial Training, 29*(3), 199-216. doi:10.1108/03090590510591085

Jung, C. G. (1933). *Modern man in search of a soul.* New York, NY, USA: Harcourt Brace Jovanovich.

Jung, C., & Hull, R. F. (1957). The Self. *CrossCurrents, 7*(3), 263-271. Retrieved from http://www.jstor.org.fgul.idm.oclc. org/stable/24456498

Karp, T., & Helgo, T. I. (2009). Leadership as identity construction: The act of leading people in organisations. *Journal of Management Development, 28*(10), 880-896. doi:10.1108/02621710911000659

Kegan, R. (1982). *Problem and process in human development.* Boston, MA: Harvard College.

Kegan, R. (1994). *In over our heads: The mental demands of modern life.* Cambridge, MA: Harvard University Press.

Kegan, R., & Lahey, L. L. (2009). *Immunity to change: How to overcome it and unlock potential in yourself and your organization.* Boston, MA: Harvard Business School.

King, S., & Nicol, D. M. (1999). Organizational enhancement through recognition of individual spirituality: Reflections of Jaques and Jung. *Journal of Organizational Change Management, 12*(3), 234-242.

Lemoine, N. B., & James, G. (2014, January). What VUCA really means for you. Retrieved from https://hbr. org/2014/01/what-vuca-really-means-for-you

Lieblich, A., Tuval-Mashiach, R., & Zilber, T. (1998). *Narrative Research: Reading, analysis and interpretation.* Thousand Oaks, CA: SAGE Publications.

McAdams, D. P. (1995). *The life story interview.* Retrieved from Northwestern University: www.sesp.northwestern.edu/docs/Interviewrevised95.pdf

McAdams, D. P. (2001). The psychology of life stories. *Review of General Psychology, 5*(2), 100-122. doi:10.1037//1089-2680.5.2.100

McCall, M. W. (2002). *Developing global executives: the lessons of international experience.* Boston: Harvard Business School Publishing.

Mendenhall, M., Osland, J., Bird, A., Oddou, G. R., & Maznevski, M. L. (2008). *Global leadership: Research, practice and development.* New York, NY: Routledge.

Merriam, S. B. (2007). *Learning in Adulthood: A Comprehensive Guide.* San Francisco: John Wiley & Sons, Inc.

Mezirow, J. (1978). *Education for perspective transformation: Women's re-entry programs in community colleges.* New York, NY: Teachers College, Columbia University.

Mezirow, J. (1978, January 1). Perspective Transformation. *Adult Education, 28*(2), 100-110. doi:10.1177/074171367802800202

Mezirow, J. (1994). Understanding transformation theory. *Adult Education Quarterly, 44*(4), 222-232.

Mezirow, J. (1998, May 1). *Adult Education Quarterly, 48*(3), 185-198. Retrieved June 17, 2018, from https://doi-org. fgul.idm.oclc.org/10.1177/074171369804800305.

Mezirow, J. (2003). Transformative Learning as Discourse. *Journal of Transformative Education, 1*(1), 58-63. Retrieved from https://doi.org/10.1177/1541344603252172

Mezirow, J. (2006). An overview over transformative learning. In P. Sutherland & J. Crowther (Eds.), *Lifelong learning: Concepts and contexts.* London, England: Routledge.

Mezirow, J. (2009). Transformative learning theory. In J. Mezirow, E.W. Taylor, & Associates (Eds.), *Transformative learning in practice.* San Francisco, CA: Jossey-Bass.

Mezirow, J., & Associates. (1991). *Fostering critical reflection in adulthood: A guide to transformative and emancipatory learning.* San Francisco, CA: Jossey-Bass.

Mezirow, J., & Associates. (2000). *Learning as transformation.* San Francisco: Jossey-Bass.

Morrow, R. A. (2002). *Reading Freire and Habermas: Critical pedagogy and transformative social change.* New York, NY: Teachers College Press.

Newman, M. (2012). Calling transformative learning into question: Some mutinous thoughts. *Adult Education Quarterly, 62*(1), 36-55. doi:10.1177/0741713610392768

Osland, J., Osland, A., Bird, A., & Oddou, G. (2007). *Expert cognition in global leaders.* Philadelphia, PA: Academy of Management.

Patton, M. (2002). *Qualitative research & evaluation methods.* (3rd ed.). Thousand Oaks, CA: Sage.

Petriglieri, G., & Stein, M. (2012). The unwanted self: Projective identification in leaders' identity work. *Organization Studies, 33*(9), 1217-1235. doi:10.1177/0170840612448158

Piaget, J. (1950). *The psychology of intelligence.* (1st English Version). London, UK: Routledge & Kegan Paul.

Pinkavova, E. (2010). Keeping our heads above water: applying Kegan's 'orders of consciousness' theory in coaching. *International Journal of Evidence Based Coaching and Mentoring*, 14-21.

Poutiantine, M. I., & Conners, D. A. (2012). The role of identity in transformational learning, teaching, and leading. *New Directions for Teaching and Learning, 130*, 67-75. doi:10.1002/5l.20018

Schapiro, S. A., Gallegos, P. V., Stashower, K., & Clark, D. F. (2017). Reflections on the 12th international transformative learning conference: Engaging at the intersections of theory and practice [Monograph]. *Journal of Transformative Education, 15*(1), 6-15. doi:10.1177/1541344616685644

Singer, J. A. (2004). Narrative identity and meaning making across the adult lifespan: An introduction. *Journal of Personality, 72*(3). Retrieved October 10, 2016

Sparks, W. L., & Repede, J. F. (2016). Human motivation and leadership: Assessing the validity and reliability of the actualized leader profile. *Academy of Educational Leadership Journal, 20*(3), 23-43. doi:1528-2643

Tucker, M. F., Bonial, R., Vanhove, A., & Kedharnath, U. (2014, March 6). Leading across cultures in the human age: An empirical investigation of intercultural competency among global leaders. *Springer Plus, 3*(127).

Turner, J., & Mavin, S. (2008). What can we learn from senior leader narratives? The strutting and fretting of becoming a leader. *Leadership & Organization Development Journal, 29*(4), 376-391. doi:10.1108/01437730810876168

Zaccaro, S. J. (2007). Trait-based perspectives of leadership. *American Psychologist, 62*(6-16), 51, 54, 90, 91.

APPENDIX A

Recruiting Brief for Potential Participants

You are invited to become part of a dissertation research project on GLOBAL LEADERS at Fielding Graduate University, Santa Barbara, California. Louise Korver, Fielding Doctoral Candidate, is a board certified, professional executive coach with Global Executive Development Partners, LLC. Louise is also an adjunct instructor in the McColl School of Business, Queens University of Charlotte (North Carolina). We would like you to consider participating in this study.

What is the point of this Research? Organizations are urgently seeking ways to identify and develop a leadership pool ready to take responsibility their global operations. This research suggests that examining the journey through which cognitive and emotional skills develop might help identify the markers of leadership ability, particularly in navigating the complex process of multinational decision making involving both people, cultures and systems within the organization. Harvard cognitive psychologist Dr. Robert Kegan has provided an exciting thread of research in cognitive reasoning and emotional capacity that allows an executive to gain perspective from complex lived experiences. Most of Kegan's models are stage theories, suggesting that there are levels of intercultural competencies (world view, social interpersonal style, and situational approach) and cognitive abilities (personality and motives) that develop over time. This research is will examine how these skills eventually become apparent in success or failure in business. This study will give timely, systematic attention to the developmental journey of senior executives of multinational organizations. This study will be among the first to identify the common experiences and traits of successful global executives.

Why is this important, and what do you get out of it? Understanding life's journey and how a person becomes capable of the demands of a senior global leadership role has a compelling basis for further study. The primary research question (*What are the markers of successful global leaders that would account for their capacity to navigate the complexity of their roles?*) is this – When and how did successful senior leaders develop the capacity, capability and competence to lead global organizations? The study will correlate an individual's leadership traits and motivations to lead across many geographies, cultures, languages, and differences, to the nature of transformative learning experiences across the lifespan. In correlating global leadership attributes to these life experiences, we expect to identify the markers. As a participant in the study, you will receive a bound copy of the book, a transcript of your life story, and your leadership profiles.

What is the Ask? Ms. Korver is asking for individual senior executives (or a leadership team) willing to share their life story in an interview. The study will take place in the summer of 2017. Individual executives may volunteer by contacting Ms. Korver directly. Executives at the second level of management will be considered if a promotion into an operating executive role is expected within the 12-month period ending June 30, 2018.

The research protocol has three parts. (1) a short demographic questionnaire, (2) a 90-minute recorded interview with Ms. Korver. The interview questions will be provided in advance, and (3) two ~100-item online inventories designed to learn more about your leadership style and global experience. The results of the demographic and inventory data will be used in correlation analysis with the interview data. Confidentiality: All participants will sign a disclosure agreement in keeping with the ethics governing academic research. This study has been pre-approved by the Institutional Review Board of Fielding Graduate University. Participants will be assigned a case number (a four-digit code, selected by the participant) and asked to create a pseudonym, which will be used to collect all data. At no time will the participant's real name be used in published materials or retained in electronic form, unless pre-approved. More information about Ms. Korver's background is available at www.gxdllc.com, or through the research website (https://louisekorver.wixsite.com/mysite), which includes more detailed information about the study. This study is being conducted as part of a dissertation program at Fielding Graduate University. Fielding Graduate University is accredited by the WASC Senior College and University Commission (WSCUC), and is a Carnegie Foundation designee for community engagement, the only graduate school in the country to be so honored. Further information about Fielding can be obtained at their website: www.fielding.edu.

Thank you for considering becoming a participant in the study.

Louise A. Korver, ABD
+1 704.308.6557
lkorver@email.fielding.edu

APPENDIX B

Participant Selection Letter

Thank you for participating in the Global Leader dissertation study. This document contains the links to each of the items to complete as a participant. If you find that you are unable to access any of the documents or links, please contact me as soon as possible at +1 704.308.6557 or via email at lkorver@ email.fielding.edu. Please be sure to return the signed Informed Consent letter to confirm your participation in the study.

You will receive a copy of your results from the Global Leader TAP and the Actualized Leader Profile. After the results of the study are complete, you will receive a table of results from the Global Experience Questionnaire showing the results of all participants in the study. You will also receive a copy of the dissertation when published in early 2018, if you desire. I look forward to meeting you and learning about your life experience as a global leader!

IMPORTANT: To protect your anonymity, please use your pseudonym and 4-digit code as your Username on the surveys. (Example: TrystanMiles0720)

Item Number (Check when completed)	Description	Link to Document
☐ 1	Informed Consent	Draft Informed Consent Letter for IF — Please return one signed copy to me.
☐ 2	Interview Questions	Korver Dissertation Research Interview (
☐ 3	Demographic Questionnaire	https://www.surveymonkey.com/r/Y5LTGD5
☐ 4	Global Experience Questionnaire	GBE - Survey of Global Business Exper — Please return one signed copy to me.
☐ 5	Global Leader TAP	https://gltap.tuckerintlassessments.com/?tapkey=zXJSLZFP
☐ 6	Actualized Leader Profile	Leadership Survey Link

APPENDIX C

Codebook

Open Coding Codebook

Codebook
Age of first job - Values related
Age of first job - work ethic
First generation college student
Negative role model
Personal
Positive role model
Security for own future
Social liberal causes
Stories mirrors personal life
Stories provides value statement
Determination
Dysfunction
Early leadership experience
Failure
First memory under age 5
Greatest challenge
Grit, prioiries, figure this out
Humble (not a lot of ego)
Important Adolescent Scene
Important adult scene
Important Childhood Scene
Influencers
International expatriation
Keeping networking contacts alive
Learning politics; naivite
Lessons Learned from Failure
Life theme
Money
Nadir experience
Negative future-health concerns
Negative future-marriage falls apart
Negative future-war
Peak experience
Personal growth (always changing, growing)
Philanthopy (quiet money; quiet politics)
Philosophy of life
Politics: Social Liberal; Fiscal Conservative
Pride in accomplishment/achievement
Public visibility; performance
Reflection on life
Retire- go into politics
Retirement
Sense of Humor-examples
Spirituality
Stories
Strong family relationships
Success
Turning Point (Transformational)
Values
Work Ethic

Codebook Sorted by Alpha and Count

Codebook	Count
Age of first job - Values related	4
Age of first job - work ethic	9
Negative role model	30
Personal	11
Positive role model	57
Security for own future	25
Social liberal causes	1
Stories mirrors personal life	18
Stories provides value statement	53
47 codes	
Determination	30
Early leadership experience	4
Failure	23
First memory under age 5	22
Greatest challenge	26
Grit, priolries, figure this out	35
Humble (not a lot of ego)	3
Important Adolescent Scene	34
Important adult scene	29
Important Childhood Scene	39
Influencers	87
International expatriation	37
Keeping networking contacts alive	7
Learning politics; naivite	20
Lessons Learned from Failure	20
Life theme	21
Money	32
Nadir experience	39
Negative future-health concerns	16
Negative future-marriage falls apart	1
Negative future-war	6
Peak experience	31
Personal growth (always changing, growing)	11
Philanthopy (quiet money; quiet politics)	17
Philosophy of life	20
Politics: Social Liberal; Fiscal Conservative	28
Pride in accomplishment/achievement	16
Public visibility; performance	8
Reflection on life	30
Retire-go into politics	1
Retirement	27
Sense of Humor-examples	10
Spirituality	49
Stories	69
Strong family relationships	21
Success	63
Turning Point (Transformational)	130
Values	107

Codebook by Count

Codebook	Count
Turning Point (Transformational)	130
Values	107
Work Ethic	95
Influencers	87
Stories	69
Success	63
Positive role model	57
Stories provides value statement	53
Spirituality	49
Important Childhood Scene	39
Nadir experience	39
International expatriation	37
Grit, prioiries, figure this out	35
Important Adolescent Scene	34
Money	32
Peak experience	31
Negative role model	30
Determination	30
Reflection on life	30
Important adult scene	29
Politics: Social Liberal; Fiscal Conservative	28
Retirement	27
Greatest challenge	26
Security for own future	25
Failure	23
First memory under age 5	22
Life theme	21
Strong family relationships	21
Learning politics; naivite	20
Lessons Learned from Failure	20
Philosophy of life	20
Stories mirrors personal life	18
Philanthopy (quiet money; quiet politics)	17
Negative future-health concerns	16
Pride in accomplishment/achievement	16
Personal	11
Personal growth (always changing, growing)	11
Sense of Humor-examples	10
Age of first job - work ethic	9
Public visibility; performance	8
Keeping networking contacts alive	7
Negative future-war	6
Early leadership experience	4
Age of first job - Values related	4
Humble (not a lot of ego)	3
Social liberal causes	1
Negative future-marriage falls apart	1
Retire-go into politics	1
	1472

APPENDIX D

Script to Exclude Potential Participants

The following script is used for excluding potential participants:

Thank you for your interest in this study of global leaders. Many potential participants contacted me to be part of the study. At this, I have filled my quota of individuals with background characteristics like yours. While you will not be able to participate in this study, I understand your interest in the general topic of global leadership success.

Since this study is part of an ongoing research program, if another research study cohort is formed, I will reach out to you. In the meantime, once this study has been approved and published, I will forward a copy of the study's bibliography and a link to the study findings.

Sincerely,

Louise A. Korver, ABD
Fielding Graduate University

APPENDIX E

Informed Consent Form

(to be completed by participants age 18 and over)
Fielding Graduate University
2020 De la Vina Street | Santa Barbara, California 93105-3814

Informed Consent Form
MARKERS OF SUCCESSFUL GLOBAL LEADERS:
WHAT ACCOUNTS FOR THEIR CAPACITY
TO NAVIGATE THE COMPLEXITY OF THEIR ROLES?

TrystanMiles0720
Via email to: trystanMiles0720@gmail.com

Dear Mr. Miles:

You have been asked to participate in a research study conducted by Louise Korver, a doctoral candidate in the School of Leadership Studies at Fielding Graduate University, Santa Barbara, CA. This study is supervised by Dr. Lenneal Henderson. This research involves the study of global leaders and is part of Ms. Korver's Fielding dissertation study. You are being contacted as a candidate for this study because your name was provided from Ann Danner, who thought you would be interested in participating.

The study involves an interview to be arranged at your convenience. This will last approximately 90 minutes. The information you provide will be kept strictly confidential. The informed consent forms and other identifying information will be kept separate from the data. All materials will be kept in North Carolina as an electronic recording and a typed transcript. The tape recordings will be listened to only by the Researcher, Dr. Lenneal Henderson, and a confidential Research Assistant, who has signed a Professional Assistance Confidentiality Agreement to protect your confidentiality. Any records that would identify you as a participant in this study, such as informed consent forms, will be destroyed by me approximately two years after the study is completed.

You will be asked to provide a different name (a pseudonym) and will be assigned a four-digit code for any quotes that might be included in the final research report. If any direct quotes using your pseudonym will be used, permission will be sought from you first. The results of this research will be published in the dissertation, subsequent journals, or books.

You may develop greater personal awareness of your leadership strengths because of your participation in this research. The risks to you are considered minimal, and there is a small chance that you may experience some emotional discomfort during or after your participation. Should you experience such discomfort, please contact a local psychologist from the list provided by the Researcher.

You may withdraw from this study at any time, either during or after your participation, without negative consequences. Should you withdraw, your data will be eliminated from the study and will be destroyed.

No compensation will be provided for participation. You may request a copy of the summary of the final results by indicating your interest at the end of this form.

If you have any questions about any aspect of this study or your involvement, please tell the Researcher before signing this form. You may also contact the supervising faculty if you have questions or concerns about your participation in this study. The supervising faculty has provided contact information at the bottom of this form.

If you have questions or concerns about your rights as a research participant, contact the Fielding Graduate University Institutional Review Board (IRB) by email at irb@fielding.edu or by telephone at 805-898-4033.

Please print two copies of this informed consent form. Kindly sign both, indicating you have read, understood, and agree to participate in this research. Return one to the researcher and keep the other for your files. The Institutional Review Board of Fielding Graduate University retains the right to access the signed informed consent forms and other study documents.

_____

NAME OF PARTICIPANT (please print)

_____

SIGNATURE OF PARTICIPANT

_____

DATE

Lenneal Henderson, Ph.D.   Louise A. Korver
Chair of the Committee   Doctoral Candidate
Fielding Graduate University   Fielding Graduate University
2112 Santa Barbara Street   16600 Redcliff Drive, Unit O
Santa Barbara, CA 93105   Huntersville, North Carolina 28078
+1-805-687-1099   +1-704-308-6557

☐ Yes, please send a summary of the study results to me.

☐ No, I do not require a summary of the study results.

_____

NAME (please print)

_____

Street Address

_____

City, State, Zip code or Country Code

_____

Country

_____

Other contact information (email/direct phone)

APPENDIX F

Caligiuri's 10 Tasks of Global Leaders[9] as a Participant Selection Tool

Tasks Performed	Scale						
	1	2	3	4	5	6	7
	Not to any extent, To a small extent, To a moderate extent, To a great extent, To a very great extent						
1. I work with colleagues from other countries.	1	2	3	4	5	6	7
2. I interact with external clients from other countries.	1	2	3	4	5	6	7
3. I interact with internal clients from other countries.	1	2	3	4	5	6	7
4. I may need to speak in a language other than their mother tongue at work.	1	2	3	4	5	6	7
5. I supervise employees who are of different nationalities.	1	2	3	4	5	6	7
6. I develop a strategic business plan on a worldwide basis for their unit.	1	2	3	4	5	6	7
7. I manage a budget on a worldwide basis for their unit.	1	2	3	4	5	6	7
8. I negotiate in other countries or with people from other countries.	1	2	3	4	5	6	7
9. I manage foreign suppliers or vendors.	1	2	3	4	5	6	7
10. I manage risk on a worldwide basis for their unit.	1	2	3	4	5	6	7

Caligiuri, 2006, p. 220

[9] Reprinted from Human Resource Management Review, 16, Paula Caligiuri, Developing global leaders, 219-228, Copyright (2006), with permission from Elsevier.

APPENDIX G

The GLTAP Social Desirability Scale Items

- I am always full of energy.
- People never disappoint me.
- I am never bored.
- I never make judgments about people based on first impressions.
- I have never met a person that I did not like.
- I have never been irritated when people expressed ideas very different from my own.
- I never hesitate to go out of my way to help someone in trouble.
- I am always courteous, even to people who are disagreeable.
- I'm always willing to admit it when I make a mistake.

(Copyright Tucker International, LLC)

APPENDIX H

The McAdams Life Story Interview Categories

1. Life Chapters
2. Critical Events (eight specific life events)
    a. Peak Experience
    b. Nadir Experience
    c. Turning Point
    d. Earliest Memory
    e. Important Childhood Scene
    f. Important Adolescent Scene
    g. Important Adult Scene
    h. One Other Important Scene
3. Life Challenge (single greatest challenge)
4. Influences on the Life Story
    a. Positive (identify the single person, group, or organization that has had the greatest positive influence on the story)
    b. Negative (identify the single person, group, or organization that has had the greatest positive influence on the story)
5. Stories and the Life Story (three specific stories)
    a. Television, Movie, Performance (stories watched)
    b. Books, Magazines (stories read)
    v. Family Stories, Friends (stories heard)

6. Alternative Futures for the Life Story
    a. Positive Future (would like to happen, including goals and dreams)
    b. Negative Future (high undesirable; you fear)
7. Personal Ideology
    a. Religious or Spiritual
        i. How these might have changed
    b. Political and Social Issues
    c. Most Important Value in Human Living
    d. Fundamental Beliefs and Values (what else?)
8. Life Theme (central theme, message, idea)
9. Other (what else?)

www.ingramcontent.com/pod-product-compliance
Lightning Source LLC
Chambersburg PA
CBHW061248280526
45784CB00002B/676